Housekeeping
Secrets

My Mother Never Taught Me

Joni Hilton

Housekeeping Secrets

My Mother Never Taught Me

PRIMA HOME

An Imprint of Prima Publishing

3000 Lava Ridge Court ✴ Roseville, California 95661

(800) 632-8676 ✴ www.primalifestyles.com

Library of Congress Cataloging-in-Publication Data
Hilton, Joni
    Housekeeping secrets my mother never taught me / Joni Hilton.
       p.   cm. — (Secrets my mother never taught me)
    Includes index.
    ISBN 0-7615-2819-9
    1. Housekeeping. I. Title. II. Series.
  TX147 .H38 2000
  648—dc21   00-058887

01 02 03 DD 10 9 8 7 6 5 4 3 2 1
Printed in the United States of America

How to Order
Single copies may be ordered from Prima Publishing, 3000 Lava Ridge Ct., Roseville, CA 95661; telephone (800) 632-8676 ext. 4444. Quan-tity discounts are also available. On your letterhead, include informa-tion concerning the intended use of the books and the number of books you wish to purchase.

Visit us online at www.primalifestyles.com

Contents

Acknowledgments

Many of the tips and tricks shared in this book were contributed by some of the cleverest people I know. Whether a longtime friend or someone I met briefly on a plane trip across country, I must give a big hug and thank you to the following dear people—superlative housekeepers all:

My husband, Bob Hilton; my mother, Coralee Pennock; Deniece Schofield, Christy Noll, Cynthia Rhine, Karen Rogers, Teru Miyashima, Jeannie Kuczewski, Dixie Albright, Aherne Del Pero, Cathi Ellington, Dara Favero, Ginger Jenkins, Ruth Landis, Gloria Morrill, Judy Ohmer, Kathy Petersen, Terry Ryan, Susan Stanley, Shelley Surratt, Mary Louise Walter, Yvonne Burch, Susan Foster, Hilary Hinckley, Debbie Newbold, Nanette Slaughter, and Kirstie Alley.

And my deep appreciation also goes to the following organizations who provided much helpful information:

Soap and Detergent Association, The Humane Society, National Burglar and Fire Alarm Association, the Federal Emergency Management Agency, the U.S. Department of Agriculture, Science and Education Administration, Mayflower

Transit, Fair Oaks Nursery, Canine College, and financial planner Dick Stoeltzing.

Last, this book would not have been possible without the genius of Prima editors Jamie Miller, Denise Sternad, and Libby Larson. Thank you all for your invaluable contributions.

Introduction

Everything Mom forgot to tell you can be found within these pages. Most moms today are either working outside the home or have little time to teach you how to sew on a button; in some cases, they've even hired someone else to do the housekeeping. Either way, the days of learning "home skills" at the elbow of one's mother are pretty much gone—along with old TV shows like *Father Knows Best*.

And yet we all want to live comfortably and beautifully and have a well-run home, right? But if you haven't been shown how to do all the little and big tasks that accomplish this goal—such as the right way to fold towels, bleach laundry, hang pictures, polish silver, and so on—where do you learn them? Right here, of course. This how-to book provides you with all the secrets and tricks of the trade, giving you basic, straightforward instructions on the best ways to decorate and keep your house clean and organized. It'll save you time by showing you how to do tasks more efficiently and effectively, and it'll save you money by showing you how to take care of all the things you own so that they last longer. You may even learn a thing or two Mom doesn't know herself. And that's a joy all its own, isn't it?

Whether you're living in a dorm, independently single, newly married, a recent homeowner, or just tired of ruining clothes every time you wash, this book will make life simpler. Your home is your domain, your springboard each morning as you head off into the world. It's the haven you return to each night. It should be a safe, clean, orderly, and attractive—possibly even classy—refuge. But when your home starts to get so messy you don't know where to begin, and you dread the sight of it—eating out night after night just to avoid the dishes and the laundry and the vacuuming—it becomes a stress producer. Rather than your home being a place of welcome, you find yourself telling friends *not* to come over or madly stuffing everything into the dishwasher if unexpected guests arrive (which, by the way, is actually a pretty good hiding spot if you are caught in such a predicament).

Conversely, when you know you're taking care of your home properly, you feel better about yourself, you breathe cleaner air, you wear crisper clothes, you actually *position* yourself to succeed in the outside world. And when you think of it that way, housekeeping becomes exhilarating, cleansing, and even creative. Take pride in your home and make it an expression of your best self.

Part One

Getting Started

Chapter One

What Constitutes a Clean House?

1f you dropped by my house unannounced one afternoon, you might expect to find an immaculate, sanitized environment where everything, including the furniture, is alphabetized. Boy, would you be in for a surprise. Is my home clean? Yep. Is it so sterile that you wonder if people live there? Not in the least. Yes, we have dust bunnies, and we chase them down like everybody else. We also have a dog and three cats who, near as I can tell, don't intend to stop shedding. We have four children who keep their rooms in varying stages of order, and who sometimes leave books, toys, homework, and jackets strewn about until they're reminded to put them away.

But I wouldn't hesitate to welcome you in because I love the spirit in our house—call it a mood, or an atmosphere, but we have a blast in the Hilton house. Comedy reigns supreme, dinnertime conversation is always lively, and visitors are welcome—

3

even when toys are still scattered and the dust bunnies seem to be multiplying. People who are too wrapped up in perfection are not a lot of fun to visit; you never feel you can relax and put your feet up. They seem to hover over you the whole time, almost dusting behind you as you leave (which you are eager to do in such homes).

It's Easier than You Think

At our house, while we maintain the basic rules of cleanliness, we also know that daily living entails a certain amount of mess, and we accept that. Whether you live in a house or an apartment, be gentle on yourself; don't aspire to have the very cleanest home you've ever seen—you'll probably go overboard trying to create it. How do you tell the difference between what's clean enough and what's being fanatical? I'll tell you. Here are the things you could expect from a professional maid service, and if you can do these yourself, your home will be officially clean.

Overall

Furniture is dusted (remember to work from top to bottom).

Hallways are swept.

Carpets are vacuumed, including under furniture.

Marks on rugs are spot-cleaned.

Baseboards are not wearing a layer of dust.

Cobwebs are gone, inside and out.

Leaves are swept from walkway and porch.

Front door is clean (no fingerprints).

Wastebaskets are emptied.

Light switches and doorknobs are wiped clean.

Exteriors of washer and dryer are wiped down.

Laundry room floor is mopped or swept.

Mirrors and windows are clean.

Wood furniture is polished.

Pillows and furniture are vacuumed and straightened.

Ledges are dusted (windowsills, bookcases, hearths).

Lampshades and pictures are dusted.

Fireplaces are clean.

Plant leaves—real or artificial—are clean.

Kitchen

Dishes are washed, as well as can opener blade.

Fronts and tops of all appliances and cabinet doors are clean.

Stove burners are clean.

Countertops and backsplashes are clean.

Inside of microwave is clean.

Sinks and faucets are clean.

Cupboard under main sink has been wiped out, disinfected.

Tip

Confine eating to the kitchen and dining room; the rest of your home will stay cleaner.

Spills in refrigerator are cleaned up.

Floor is swept or mopped.

Chair cushions and rugs are cleaned.

Any furniture or wall hangings are dusted.

Bathrooms

All shampoo, toothpaste, and toiletries are in proper place.

Tub and shower walls are scrubbed.

Inside and outside of toilet is clean.

Mirrors and light fixtures are clean.

Countertops and sink are clean.

Floors are mopped.

Walls, especially around light switches, are clean.

Towels are clean, hung straight.

Bedrooms

Laundry, sheets, and bedding washed weekly.

Belongings arranged neatly.

Clothes and shoes in appropriate places.

Bed frame, lamps, pictures, dressers, and desk are all dusted.

Mirrors cleaned.

Wood furniture polished.

Floor vacuumed, including under bed.

Blinds dusted if necessary.

That's it. And most maid services do not include windows or laundry. If you can check off the above items, your house will be—and smell—perfectly clean. Of course, there are big jobs that you'll need to do on occasion—vacuuming refrigerator coils, cleaning out bookcases, cleaning the oven, filing recipes,

Listen to Your Mother!

There are many cleaning fanatics in this world, and I always wonder how they sleep at night, knowing minute particles of dust are slowly settling onto the tops of their curtains. These are people who vacuum their mattresses twice a day, iron every sheet and pillowcase they wash, scrub the bathroom floor during commercial breaks, and pick lint out of the carpet with tweezers.

Do not be like this. Allow your house to look lived in—not every phone cord has to recoil into a decorative plastic box, out of view. Not everybody who comes over is check-ing to see if the fringe on your rug is all combed in one direction. Your personal sense of self-worth should not depend on having Lysol sprayed on every surface. Relax. You want a well-ordered, clean home, but you won't be conducting open-heart surgery in your living room or making dust-free computer chips. Use the list in this chapter to establish a basic guideline for what constitutes a clean house, then relax about the rest of the stuff, doing it when you can. You should enjoy your home, and that means striking a balance between "clean enough" and "fanatically sterile."

polishing silver, and so on—but for a *basic* cleaning, the above list is sufficient. Anybody in this world could visit your home and you could beam with pride.

Hiring a Housekeeper

I have had some of the worst housekeepers in the world. I've also had some of the best. I've had live-in help, once-a-week maids, and nothing at all (except the combined efforts of my own family). Guess who actually does the best job?

You do. You will never find a housekeeper who has exactly your standards and your way of doing things—she won't shake the crumbs out of the toaster, she won't put the strainer where you like it, she won't dust behind the grandfather clock, and she won't leave the mantel stuff turned at the angle you like. (In my case, she may even pour Clorox on an oriental rug.) Something, trust me, something will bug you.

Having a maid doesn't magically guarantee you a perfect house, and if you're considering hiring one, you need to weigh the pros and cons carefully. For instance, if you're raising a family, kids will immediately drop their standards of cleanliness and order because they know the maid is coming and she'll take care of it. When kids—and adults, for that matter—are responsible for sweeping up the floors and shining the faucets, believe me, they keep things cleaner in the first place. So, even if you can afford it, can you afford it?

On the other hand, I have to admit that it's a tremendous help to have help. When somebody pops in and does the basics for you, it does give you more personal time. And you can lavish that on those you love or on other pursuits. Just be sure you still assign chores and teach housekeeping skills to your children.

Listen to Your Mother!

If you do choose to hire some help, interview carefully, check references, and follow your hunches. This person needs to be a good match with your personality, not just a good cleaner. Your phone book will list agencies that provide domestic help, and they can explain all the legal requirements as well, such as labor laws and the taxes you may need to pay.

When you finally hire someone, be very clear about what you expect him or her to do; the opportunity for miscommunication is high here, and you want to give explicit instructions. Some women feel embarrassed in the boss role and hesitate to ask too much of a maid. But housekeepers would prefer that you make your needs known—wouldn't you rather work on an assignment you clearly understand than one vaguely explained? Let your housecleaner know the things that matter most to you. Be respectful, of course, and don't bark out orders; just be natural, friendly, and clear. In other words, be yourself.

And don't clean the house before she or he comes! Housekeepers expect to be needed, so don't be embarrassed and tidy up. Besides, there's a sense of satisfaction for those who clean if they can see a difference afterward. Cleaning homes is indeed a very respectable task—maids work hard and help you order your life on its most intimate terms. You place them in a high position of trust. Their work is anything but menial; it's as if you've hired a personal assistant. Which is all the more reason to choose carefully when you hire; you're really picking a teammate.

Live-in help gives you the freedom to run out in the evening for a piece of pie with your husband, knowing you don't have to hire a sitter. On the other hand, some people (usually men) feel their privacy is diminished when you hire someone who lives with you, if only because most husbands want to lounge around in a robe and read the paper without feeling guilty for not being dressed yet. Depending on the size of your home, you can arrange separate quarters so privacy is maximized. But many people love the camaraderie live-in help provides: working together to chop things in the kitchen, laughing with somebody at the cute things kids do, oftentimes the chance for everyone to learn a second language, and even knowing somebody is always at home for security purposes.

Last, but most important, treat employees well. Express sincere appreciation and genuine admiration, and you'll develop a relationship that may last a lifetime.

Chapter Two

Finding Time

Finding the time to keep a house clean can be the hardest part of housekeeping. I find it helpful to choose a realistic schedule that I can stick to. Okay, at least most of the time.

Choosing a Schedule

You need a housekeeping schedule that works for you. Lots of people like the unhurried feeling of sprucing up on a Saturday morning. But if you can't bear to spend weekend time on housekeeping, choose an evening and block out a couple of hours to zip through and get everything done. Don't be afraid to choose an unorthodox schedule, as long as it works for you. Some people have insomnia, and that's when they get up and clean the house. Others clean house for fifteen minutes every morning instead of (or in addition to) exercising. Cleaning a little at a time works for some people. Another idea is to pick up clutter and do dishes before you go to bed, then at least you have some semblance of order each night. I like to sweep through the entire house in one massive, weekly cleaning. Then I know that at least once a week the whole house is totally spotless. Choose a style that fits your personality and life.

Get Moving

Next, clean fast. Put on some upbeat music and get moving. What makes cleaning seem like drudgery is when you plod along, wring out clothes one drip at a time, and crawl through the experience with eyes half closed. The way to enjoy it is to pick up the pace and feel you've accomplished a lot in a short time. You'll finish sooner and feel more invigorated. You could even make a game or contest out of it: Set a time limit and see how much you can do in thirty minutes, an hour, and so on.

Delegate

If you don't live alone, you absolutely must share duties with everyone in your house, whether there are two of you or ten. Everyone contributed to the dirt and mess, right? So everyone must pitch in. And believe me, once you have children, this is a lesson you must teach early—everybody has a job to do. Otherwise you're picking up after a growing family and your resentment will grow right along with them. Divide up the chores and trade off each week if some task is particularly distasteful to everyone. Post a chart if it helps you stay organized and know whose job it is to take out the trash, clean out the fridge, and so on.

If you're the parent of young children, you can draw up a chart, and use magnets or popsicle sticks to rotate which person has which set of duties, making sure the little ones rotate among themselves, so they aren't suddenly climbing ladders or trying to move sofas. In a household of adults, a household meeting is a good idea, so that everyone can contribute what they feel is a fair distribution of the assignments, and a reasonable time limit for each person.

A good rule of thumb is that nobody's done 'til the work is done. If you finish early, be a good guy and help a slower member of the team with her chores. To prevent resentment if someone isn't doing their job, attach a reward for those who finish on time. With dawdling children, sometimes you have to withhold a privilege until their tasks are completed.

Finding More Time

What if you simply don't have time to clean? We all think we're so busy that there isn't one spare minute in the day, but there are ways to find more time if we're willing to adjust our routines a little.

Get and stay organized. Clutter makes us rummage, and that eats up valuable time. Throw away or donate the items you haven't used in a year, and put the rest where they are most frequently used. Clean out junk areas, and put everything in order. Use storage containers and labels. Believe me, you will save hours of time that you used to spend hunting for lost items. This topic is worth a whole book in and of itself, and there are many good ones.

✳ Joni's Favorites ✳

There are many books on organizing. I like Deniece Schofield's *Springing the Family Time Trap* (1997), and her *Confessions of an Organized Homemaker* (Better Way Books, 1994).

Limit phone time. Keep a clock near the phone and choose a reasonable time for chatting. Then say good-bye. Another smart idea is to keep a project by the phone so you can work as you speak—this could be any kind of mending, handwork, polishing, envelope stamping—things that don't require much concentration.

Exercise so you'll need less sleep. If you could get by with an hour less sleep, just imagine all you could accomplish—besides housekeeping!

Run errands in clumps. Don't drive to the video store, come home, go back out to the dry cleaners, then crisscross town for office supplies. Group your errands by location and run four or five in one day. Plan ahead, jotting on your calendar when you'll need to pick up film, stop by the pharmacy, and so on. You'll not only save time but gasoline.

Tip

Turn off the TV. Even if you shorten your television viewing by only thirty minutes a day, you can make your home sparkle in that half an hour.

Monitor what you read, the movies you watch, and your use of the computer. Sometimes we fill our minutes with celebrity trivia, pulp fiction, and worse. Choose to pursue only what really uplifts you or educates. Discard the rest, and you'll be amazed at how much extra time you suddenly have.

Don't window shop. Unless you're power-walking through the mall for exercise, window shopping is a big time gobbler. Know what you want before you go shopping, make the comparison phone calls necessary, then get in and get out.

Use your commute time, if you can. Carpool or take a bus or train to work, so you can catch up on necessary reading and paperwork. You'll take less work home and have more time to enjoy (and clean) your home surroundings.

Keep a calendar and write down all appointments, weddings, sales, parties, and other notifications that come in the mail. Then throw the mail away.

Listen to Your Mother!

Here are some "clean as you go" strategies: Hang up clothes, make your bed, and put away accessories as you use them. Don't kick off shoes anywhere; put them where they belong. In the kitchen, after preparing food, wipe the counter clean of crumbs and spills. Rinse and put your dishes in the dishwasher. Wipe down the sink. If you track in mud on your shoes, get a wet paper towel and mop it up right away. If you plop down on the sofa to read, take your reading materials with you when you get up and then put them away. After watching TV, straighten cushions and pillows.

Don't let dirt accumulate in the first place. You'll find that keeping things clean as you go takes almost no time at all, but if you don't, you'll have to block out hours of time to do what could have already been done.

In short, take a look at your typical, full-to-the-brim week and find ways to make space here and there for the necessary cleaning chores. Most people only need three or four hours a week to get it all done, and if you have a small place and work fast, you might need even less. Once you've established cleaning into your everyday routine, doing your chores will become natural and second nature, and you will enjoy your fun time—whether at home or away—even more.

Cleaning as You Go

The easiest way to keep a house clean is to keep a clean house. That is, when you use the bathroom, don't splash the counters and mirror, yank off a towel to dry your hands, and leave the mess for the next person to find. Instead, make this your home's policy: leave no trace that you were there. If you use the bathroom, check the toilet to make sure it looks just as clean as when you walked in. Close the lid. After you use the sink, wipe down any water that splashes on the counter or mirror. Hang the towels straight as you leave. Voila! There's a bathroom that needs no touching up. This is a great mentality to have when you're a houseguest, and it makes just as much sense at home, too. It's being considerate of the next person, but it makes life more pleasant even if you live alone.

Chapter Three

Tools of the Trade

Just as you can't ski on two-by-fours, you can't keep your house or apartment clean if you have the wrong equipment. Having the right tools and products will make it infinitely easier to do the job right. So treat this chapter as a shopping list. Here are all the basic tools and products you'll need to clean your home, along with descriptions of what they're used for.

A good all-purpose cleaner—This is the (usually white) plastic bottle with the pump-spray that can be used on just about every surface except wood. You may be familiar with brands such as Fantastic, 409, or Simple Green. These are great for getting counters and walls clean (especially for removing fingerprints around light switches), and even for spritzing rubber tennis shoes, purses, stainless steel, painted surfaces, toys, and anything plastic or vinyl. Be careful using it on walls, since it sometimes rubs off paint (test first in an inconspicuous area). Look for

> **Tip**
>
> To save money, buy cleaning products in bulk, then pour them into spray bottles as needed (be sure to label).

wet wipes containing all-purpose cleaner, too, and store under the kitchen sink.

Glass cleaner—Good ol' blue Windex and similar brands are essential not only for windows and glass objects but for mirrors, too. Another good way to clean windows is with vinegar diluted with water. I like to keep one under the kitchen sink and one under each bathroom sink, just to save steps.

> **Tip**
> Glass cleaner also helps take rings off your fingers if you have a hard time removing one.

Laundry detergent—Choose powder, liquid, or a concentrate, whichever you prefer. Store laundry products by your washing machine or, if you use a laundromat, store these products where you gather your dirty clothes—by a hamper.

Bleach—Yup, scary as it sounds. Chlorine bleach is used not just for making dull laundry white again (see chapter 5), but when it's super-diluted (1 cup of bleach for every gallon of water) in a spray bottle, it's a great disinfectant for bathrooms, kitchen counters, garbage cans—you name it. A capful in your toilet tank will prevent rust marks and rings. If you prefer to use a disinfectant such as Lysol, be sure to keep it on hand and spray generously on phones, in sinks, and around keyboards and toilets to keep them germ-free.

Fabric softener—This isn't strictly necessary, but I like the scented sheets that you can toss into the dryer. (And used sheets are great for shining chrome faucets, by the way.) To save money, make your own sheets by dampening a washcloth with liquid fabric softener, and adding that to your dryer. If you prefer liquid fabric softener, which is used in the washing machine, some machines will automatically add it for you. Otherwise, you'll have to watch the time and add it when your wash begins the rinse cycle. Some people object to the gradual build-up of softeners on clothes. And I don't add them to a load of rags because then the rags will be less absorbent. But for clothes I like the softness, the scent, and the static-free results.

Dishwashing liquid—If you have a dishwasher, you'll need two kinds of dish soap: one for hand washing dishes in the sink, and dishwasher soap made for machines. Make sure you don't confuse them—if you use hand-washing dish soap in the automatic machine, you'll wind up with a kitchen floor covered with suds, not to mention possible plumbing problems. For sink use, I like to buy the kind of dishwashing liquid in a pump dispenser that's also a liquid soap for washing hands.

Dusting polish—Read the labels and get one that doesn't build up a thick, waxy coating that will dull your furniture. Keep it in your cleaning caddy (see page 21).

Oven cleaner—Get this unless you have a self-cleaning oven. Store under the kitchen sink.

By the way, store metal spray cans on a rubber mat or in a plastic caddy to prevent circular rust marks on your cabinetry. Plastic lids from frosting, margarine tubs, and the like that are a bit larger than the can make good "coasters" for this purpose.

Tip: WD-40 is great for removing crayon marks from painted walls.

Nonscratch cleaner—This is for tubs, tiles, and sinks that a harsh cleanser would scratch. It comes in similar bottles to the all-purpose cleaner listed above. Store under bathroom sink. Some contain chemicals that help eliminate mildew or lime deposits.

Oil for squeaky hinges—WD-40 and similar products help you repair as you go. Keep in your cleaning caddy.

Ladder or step stool—If you have areas you cannot reach, hey, they aren't going to clean themselves. Fold and store a step ladder in a closet or garage. (And someday, if you hire a maid, she's going to be short. Believe me, this is Murphy's Law in action; housekeepers can never reach high enough.)

Carpet stain removers—Whether removing pet, food, or dirt marks, you need a good product to keep rugs unspotted. For pet stains, I like Nature's Miracle. For regular carpet cleaning, I've had good results with Chem Dry, Woolite, and Folex.

Spot removers for clothing—Hair spray or club soda will remove ballpoint pen marks. But you'll need an overall spot-treatment solution for doing laundry, too. Spray 'n Wash and Wisk are great. I keep some spot removers in my clothes closet and dab on a stick stain-remover before I toss the soiled item into the hamper. Overall laundry solution spot removers are kept by the washing machine.

Shower spray cleaners—These really work on glass and tile and save a lot of trouble if you use them daily. Keep in the shower and use after you shower. A quick spritz on the walls will do it.

An applicator filled with house paint—Chipped or scratched wooden cupboards, drawers, floorboards, and walls won't look right no matter how much you clean them. To keep the paint job looking new, dab a little matching paint on the spot with an old shoe polish bottle or a squeeze bottle and sponge. If you're not sure of the color, take a sample to a paint store; they have a machine

✳ Joni's Favorites ✳

I like Zout, K2R, and Energine for removing spots from garments that otherwise have to make a trip to the cleaners.

✳ Joni's Favorites ✳

For keeping the shower glass and tile clean, I like the Clean Shower brand.

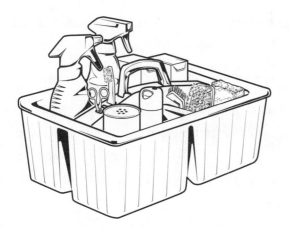

that "reads" the swatch and comes up with an instant matching formula. (If your surfaces are wood grain, there are markers you can buy specifically for camouflaging scrapes.) Tote it in your cleaning caddy for touching up as you go. I recommend touching up chipped paint even if you rent an apartment, when technically the landlord should do it. You're the one who has to live with those nicks and scratches, and a landlord may not make it a priority. So go ahead and keep your place sparkling.

A cleaning caddy—Get a caddy or tote with a plastic handle and put all your cleaning stuff in it. Not only will this keep everything neatly stored under a sink, but it makes it easier to carry the products to where you need them.

> Tip
> If you have mini-blinds, cotton work gloves are a godsend—just put them on and get them sudsy, then wipe the blinds with your gloved hands.

Another option, if you have space, is a rolling cart. These hold more and are easier on your back. If you have a large home or multiple levels, it makes sense to keep several caddies where you'll need them.

Rubber gloves—You can make do without them, but if you want to save your hands and fingernails, gloves are the way to go. I keep mine in the caddy.

Toilet bowl brush—You need to clean your toilet with a tool that is not used on anything else. Look for the curved ones that make it easier to clean under the rim. Replace when bristles are bent and less effective, just as you would replace a toothbrush. This brush needs a separate receptacle under the sink, where it is stored out of view, and where germs cannot contaminate other cleaning implements. (If your toilet has developed a stubborn ring, use a pumice stone on it.)

Joni's Favorites

For cleaning the toilet bowl, I use Lysol Plus Bleach. It has an angled neck to make under-rim cleaning easier.

Toilet bowl cleaner—This is a separate product from all the others; you can't just use a general-purpose spray here. Store under the bathroom sink.

Plunger—Alas, we all need a plunger now and then (isn't that Shakespeare?). Trust me, you don't want to be caught without one when the need arises. As with the toilet bowl brush, make sure it's stored separately from other tools, with a drip pan of its own.

Broom and dustpan—Get a dustpan that snaps onto the broom handle so you'll always have them together. Store in a broom or vacuum closet, a front closet, a garage, or wherever is most convenient for you.

Tip

Cut fingers off old rubber gloves and stretch them over broom handles so they'll stay put where you lean them.

I recommend having at least two kinds of brooms, especially if you have wood floors. The first kind is a small push broom made of cloth instead of straw, which is perfect for pushing across wood floors. A great alternative is a Swiffertype broom with a flat surface that you wrap with liners. These pick up an amazing amount of dust. Pledge Grab-It is a good brand, also, and I like the DustAll cloth refills.

The second kind of broom is a straw or nylon bristle broom—angled to help you get into corners. These are more durable and are ideal for working on porches and walkways.

Squeegee—These are the best way to clean windows, mirrors, shower doors, the tile around tubs, and car windows. Store with your window cleaner.

Paper towels—And plenty of them.

For general, all-purpose cleaning, I use diluted Clorox, Fantastic, 409, Simple Green, Lysol, and Mr. Clean Wipes.

A great product I love to recommend is the disinfecting wipes such as those made by Clorox and Mr. Clean. You pull one, like a baby wipe, and use it to clean any surface you'd normally spray and wipe. Then toss them in the trash. What could be cleaner?

Trash bags—Whether you use paper or plastic, always have plenty on hand. Take one with you as you clean for the inevitable papers and junk you'll find along the way.

A bucket—You'll use this a thousand times: mopping the floor, presoaking laundry, washing the car, scrubbing anything. Store under a sink or in the laundry area.

A mop—Unless every surface in your home is carpeted, you'll need to mop floors. Like almost anything, the commercial grade string mops will be superior to the less durable products available in dime stores, and it pays to invest in quality cleaning tools. But sponge mops can work, too; just be sure to get one that has its own squeegee attached, so you can press the water out easily. Replace when signs of wear make cleaning more difficult. Store with your broom.

A vacuum cleaner—You should have two kinds: a large, upright carpet vacuum and a hand-held type for crumbs, corners, and places the big vacuum can't reach.

Rags—Use cloth diapers, old T-shirts and towels, dust cloths—the older and more lint-free, the better. You'll use them for cleaning, but also for drying wet surfaces, such as rubbing down patio furniture that you've hosed off. Toss dirty ones in the laundry, then fold and store them after they dry. Keep one or two in your caddy, and store the rest in a basket or bucket in your laundry room.

Sponges—You'll learn the kind you prefer as you clean; some people like the Scotch Brite sponges with stiff backings for scrubbing. Keep them in your caddy. Only use a sponge if you can control the bacteria it will spread if it isn't kept clean; this means microwaving it for at least a minute to kill germs (dishwashers don't get it quite hot enough).

For cleaning dishes, if you elect not to use a sponge, use a dish cloth, and toss one into the laundry basket each day. A scrub brush with a long handle is also a good way to clean dishes before loading them into the dishwasher

For other cleaning, such as in the bath, if you don't want to use a sponge, use paper towels—or a cleaning rag that you can launder when you're done.

Tip: Prevent unraveling of a string or ribbon by dabbing ends with clear nail polish.

Brushes—Various scrub brushes are essential. I like one for dishes, another for the shower, one for floors, another for cobwebs, and even old toothbrushes for woodwork and carpet edges. Like all tools and gadgets, store them where you're going to use them most frequently. I keep several in my caddy.

Steel wool pads—For scouring pots and pans, you'll need a serious cleaning agent, such as S.O.S. or Brillo. Keep under the kitchen sink.

Iron and ironing board—Most clothes will come out of the dryer wrinkle-free (and consider this when shopping—cotton and linen wrinkle most easily). But some clothes require a touch-up and others, such as a cotton blouse or shirt, require full pressing attention. Even if you think you won't need one, get a small set. You never know when you're going to pull a blazer from the closet and find that its lapel got squished the wrong way and needs a quick steaming.

✳ Joni's Favorites ✳

For a catalog of household supplies try Home Trends at
1-800-810-2340

Wood cleaners—Use this for cleaning wood. If you have hardwood floors, they need more than a periodic sweeping. Products, such as Murphy's Oil Soap, that are made just for wood can really get them clean. Store under the kitchen sink.

Laundry basket—Keep one in your closet and use it as a hamper. Use two if you have room and want to separate the whites from the colored clothes ahead of time. A basket makes it easier to haul everything back and forth to the washing machines, too. (In a pinch, wrap soiled clothes in a towel or pillowcase, and haul them that way.)

Feather duster—This is for reaching high, such as for light fixtures, fan blades, tops of tall furniture, tops of curtains, and picture frames. A feather duster will get into crevices that dusting cloths won't. It may simply knock the dust to the floor where you can then vacuum it up, but at least you won't be collecting a layer of dust on your picture frames and lampshades.

An ostrich feather duster costs more but is definitely worth it, as the feathers have little "dust-catching" barbs that really do capture the dust (then you can shake the dust off outside). Either store with your broom or in the cleaning caddy.

Other essentials—You may not use these items specifically for cleaning, but make sure you have a good supply of them. Purchase light bulbs, batteries, toilet paper, a first-aid kit, a tool kit and nails, sturdy string, packing tape, scissors, and a flashlight. More will be said about these items later in the book.

How to Make Your Own Cleaning Products

Here are some great ways to make your own excellent cleaning products—and you'll save a ton of money, too! However, before you start mixing chemicals, always make sure to wear rubber gloves and take safety precautions. And *never* mix ammonia and bleach. Those two chemicals produce a gas called chloramine that can damage your lungs. And when working with turpentine, work in an open area away from flame.

Finally, remember to label all your concoctions!

All-Purpose Cleaner

1-quart jar with lid
¼ cup trisodium phosphate (available at paint stores)
¼ cup ammonia (optional)
hot water

Mix trisodium phosphate and ammonia, then add enough hot water to fill the jar. Shake well. Just as with any strong cleaner, you can dilute this further, if you wish, for wiping down counters, showers, and so on.

Note: I can't stand the smell of ammonia, so I leave it out. You can, too.

Glass Cleaner

¼ cup ammonia
¼ cup rubbing alcohol
3½ cups warm water

Shake well in a spritz bottle—a 24 oz. bottle is a good size.

Store in lidded jars, then pour onto a rag when ready to use. Labeling is a must. Keep all products stored out of children's reach.

Dusting Polish

Mix equal parts paraffin oil and turpentine (both available at hardware stores).

Wood Polish for Shine

Mix one tablespoon of lemon oil with a quart of mineral oil (available at a pharmacy) and apply with a soft cloth.

Floor Polish

Mix one part turpentine with five parts paraffin oil (available at hardware stores).

Carpet Cleaner

1 cup Ivory soap flakes
2 tablespoons ammonia
3 cups water

In a large bowl, beat mixture until it forms a paste. Brush over spotted area. When dry, vacuum, then rinse with a damp cloth. Brush gently.

Silver Cleaner

> **Tip**
>
> To clean copper, use ketchup! It works—honestly—as does taco sauce or anything with tomato acids in it. Vinegar and salt work, too.

Use baking soda rubbed on with a damp cloth. Or, immerse silver in a porcelain pot of boiling water and a large piece of aluminum foil. For each quart of water, add 2 teaspoons baking soda and 1 teaspoon salt. Simmer one minute and remove silver with tongs. Rinse.

Part Two

Getting Down to Business

Chapter Four

Laundry

Laundry is one of the most intimidating tasks for people newly on their own. For one thing, Mom usually did it. And for another, even if you did do some, you know in your heart you probably didn't do it right. You wander down the detergent aisle mystified by all the products and how to use them. (It took a college roommate to finally convince me that I could hand wash my sweaters instead of sending them all to the cleaners.)

But if you have all the stuff discussed in chapter three, you have everything you need to do a super job. Laundry becomes a no-brainer in a hurry. If your washer and dryer are in your home, you can let loads run while you accomplish other tasks. If you find yourself waiting in a laundromat, you can bring along paperwork to finish there.

Gathering the Wash

First we'll deal with dirty clothes, and we'll discuss linens later. The best way to collect dirty clothes as they are created is in a ventilated hamper; the regular large baskets and plastic laundry baskets work fine. Do not stuff everything into a pillowcase or drawer, as air won't be able to circulate, and trapped moisture will encourage mildew.

Divide your white clothes from the colored pieces; these will be washed separately. White clothes can take whitening bleach and higher heat, while colored clothes (especially new ones) might "bleed" onto surrounding items when they get wet. Double-check care labels and make sure your clothes can be machine washed. If not, follow dry-cleaning or hand-washing instructions.

You may also want to divide your clothes by fabric types, as some synthetics can't take the heat that cottons and denims can. It's much smarter to do two small loads of like-sorted clothes than one big load that ruins half the items.

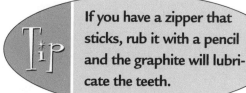

If you have a zipper that sticks, rub it with a pencil and the graphite will lubricate the teeth.

Remember to close zippers, fasten hooks, and empty pockets. One small piece of chewing gum or lipstick can ruin an entire wardrobe. And you can quote me. (Let's not even talk about chocolate Kisses or marking pens.)

Never Wash

Some items should never go into the wash. Stuffed animals and certain pillows will stay soggy too long, and lose their shape. Sofa cushion covers are best sent to the dry cleaner's, or they can shrink, ripple, and fray. Any garment with intricate embroidery, sequins, beading, or appliques should be dry-cleaned, just to be on the safe side. And don't try to wash leather or suede; take them to your dry cleaner. Ties should be dry-cleaned, also. Clothes made of rayon cannot be tossed into the dryer or they will shrink several sizes.

Wash with Caution

Tennis shoes can be machine washed; just be careful with bleach, as it can yellow and crack the rubber soles. Baseball caps can also be laundered (there's even a little basket to help them hold their shape, which can be run through the dishwasher), and curtains can be washed IF they're single-layer, simple curtains such as ones you made yourself from a sheet. Anything lined should go the cleaner's, as the lining might shrink differently than the exterior. Keep this in mind when cleaning jackets, also. If you have a lightweight, single-layer jacket, or a winter parka, you can wash it just like a shirt. But if it's a tailored, silk-lined suit coat, take it to the cleaner's. Cotton work gloves can be washed; leather ones cannot. Canvas bags can be washed; leather ones cannot. Small rugs (not oriental ones) can be washed if they fit comfortably in your machine. Otherwise, seek out professional rug cleaners.

Tip

Clean stuffed animals by shaking them in a bag with a cup of cornstarch.

Always check the label for care instructions. Every piece of clothing sold in the U.S. must carry such a label. If you can't find it at the neck, look down the side seams. If it says no chlorine bleach, there's a good reason!

Pretreating

This is also the time to examine your clothes for overlooked stains or tough grime. Mild marks, or perspiration on cuffs and collars, can be spritzed or rubbed with products such as Spray 'n Wash, or even simple shampoo. But tougher stains will need more attention (see "Stain Removal Tips"). And that brings us to pretreatment.

Here's the deal on presoaking: unless you have ground-in dirt, stubborn stains, or white clothes that have begun to gray (like tube socks), you can skip presoaking guilt-free. Just wash 'n' dry, Honey. But if you have a few items that need more attention, simply use the presoak setting on your washing machine or use your trusty bucket. Pour in ¼ cup bleach to 1 gallon of cool water (or use a commercial enzyme presoak product). Mix the bleach and water before adding clothes, as bleach is too strong to pour on them directly. This is why so many people are scared of bleach. They've seen bleach-splattered clothes unevenly bleached blue jeans, and they're scared it's just too risky— they don't want their clothes to look like a tie-dye disaster. Now, if you poured full-strength bleach directly onto your clothes, you would have reason to worry. But if it's evenly diluted in a tub or bucket of water, you'll love the results— bright, clean, new-looking clothes. However, never use chlorine bleach on wools or silks.

Tip: If you get shoe polish on your clothes, you can remove it with rubbing alcohol.

Now add your socks, undies, whatever looks dingy, and let them soak for a while, and "a while" could mean five minutes or two hours, depending on how stubborn and dark your stains are. If you're using a bucket, next dump out the bleach/water mixture and wash your clothes as usual. Bleaching too often can turn clothes yellowish, and it breaks down the fabric's fibers, so don't get overzealous about bleaching; use moderation. I once had a housekeeper who weekly blasted holes through the boys' cotton briefs, and she must have used—I swear—a quart of Clorox every time she did laundry. I think the kids just thought underwear wasn't meant for more than one or two wearings.

Many colored clothes need occasional bleaching, too, and some can even handle chlorine bleach (test first). There are several color-safe, all-fabric bleaches on the market that you can use to brighten colored clothes.

Tip Another way to get socks, underwear, or T-shirts extra white is to boil them with a few slices of lemon. Toothpaste and a small brush will clean up tennis shoes.

To keep colored clothes from fading in the first place, soak new items in salt water overnight. Or, add a cup of vinegar to their first wash cycle.

Should you hand wash all bras, pantyhose, and underwear? Nah. Some people do this, and then let them drip dry in the bathroom, but I like to zip them into a mesh bag (or you could tie them in a pillowcase) and throw them in with everything else. I toss them in the dryer, too. What can I say? It saves time.

Incidentally, to prevent runs in your stockings, dampen and freeze them when you first buy them. Thaw them (in a sink or tub), dry them, and they'll last much longer. A light spray of starch will also help them resist runs. If you already have a run, clear nail polish or hair spray will stop it in its tracks.

Stain Removal Tips

Knowing how to remove stains will save you a fortune. First, you won't have to take the item to the cleaners, and second, you won't have to replace your clothing. All of the following tricks work best if you attack the stain as quickly as possible—if you let it sit or launder the garment first, you may not have good results. Work from the inside out on your garment—don't rub the stain in further. Use a rag under where you're working, to absorb the stain and whatever you're using to remove it. Work in a well-ventilated area. To prevent spot-remover rings, blend the edges of your work with feathery strokes. And always test cleaners on a seam allowance first. If you're just not sure what to do, take it to the cleaners to be on the safe side.

Alcoholic beverages—Soak in cold water with a few drops of glycerine (available in pharmacies). Rinse with vinegar and water.

Antiperspirants—Use white vinegar, then detergent and a warm rinse.

Ballpoint pen—Use hair spray, club soda, or cleaning fluid.

Blood and meat juices—Use cold water or diluted ammonia (remember, don't mix ammonia with chlorine bleach). Cleaning fluid will sometimes help, as will a paste of water and meat tenderizer. A friend of mine uses hydrogen peroxide, then washes the garment as usual.

★ Joni's Favorites ★

Some of my favorite commercial stain removers are Energine, Zout, Shout Wipes, and Spray 'n Wash Stain Stick.

Chocolate—Use cold water, then cleaning fluid if necessary.

Coffee or tea—Presoak in a hot, diluted bleach solution.

Cranberry or beet juice and red wine—Don't let it dry. Pull fabric taut, and flush with hot water (even boiling). If dry, re-wet and apply salt, then hot water.

Crayon—Use cleaning fluid.

Fruit—Do not use soap; it will set stains. Use prewash stain remover.

Gelatin or punch—Pat with a mild ammonia solution, or rub in salt.

Glue—Sponge with acetone.

Grass stains—Soak overnight in enzyme prewash solution. Or soak in cool water, then apply cleaning fluid and detergent. Launder.

Greases, oils, butter, gravies, and dressings—Use prewash stain remover or cleaning fluid and then launder; or dampen stain with salt dissolved in ammonia and rinse; or sprinkle the stain with talcum powder to absorb the grease.

> **Tip**
> Floor wax will protect shoes and handbags, and keep them shiny.

Gum—Freeze it or dab with ice until frozen and scrape off.

Hair dye—Try shampoo, hair spray, or Zout.

Ketchup—Use prewash stain remover.

Lipstick and makeup—Cleaning fluids, such as Energine, will put greasy stains into suspension and possibly hide them. Vaseline might work also, or sponge the area with denatured alcohol and then dishwashing liquid and launder.

Mildew—Rub in lemon juice and salt, and let dry in sun. When laundering, add ½ cup disinfectant.

Mustard—Rub detergent into stain, presoak, then launder.

Nail polish—Good luck. Try nail polish remover, then wash. If mark remains, try denatured alcohol mixed with a few drops of ammonia.

Old stains—Try a dab of glycerine to soften it, then wash.

Paint—If water-based, wash with detergent in hot water. If oil-based, sponge with turpentine or paint remover first.

Pencil—Use ammonia.

Perfume spots—Use rubbing alcohol (pretest, especially on delicate fabrics).

Perspiration—Sponge with detergent and warm water, apply ammonia, and rinse. If stains are old, flush with vinegar, then rinse. Launder as usual. Some folks prefer soaking the garment in salt water, or rubbing in a paste of water and baking soda, then washing normally. If odor persists, sponge with clear mouthwash. (You can prevent such stains by using dress guards under your clothing.)

Rust—Use a purchased commercial rust remover.

Scorches—Presoak in hot, diluted bleach for five minutes. Launder. Or cover with a cloth dampened with hydrogen peroxide and iron it again. Rinse.

Shoe polish—Dab with rubbing alcohol.

Soft drinks—Sponge with cold water and alcohol.

Tar—Rub with kerosene, then launder.

Wine—Sprinkle with salt, then soak in cool water, then soak in bleach and hot water. Launder as usual.

Wax—Scrape off with a dull knife, then iron remaining wax between layers of bathroom tissues or paper towels. The tissue will absorb the melting wax. Sponge with cleaning fluid if any wax remains, then presoak if necessary. (And stop blowing out dinner candles—get a candle snifter!)

Washing

Okay, you're standing in front of the washing machine. Which cycle should you select? I know, I know—life is full of tough decisions, and here is one more. To simplify the whole thing, most washers offer you three basic cycles:

1. Permanent Press. This is for, you'll never believe it, permanent press (use any water temperature and a cold rinse if possible).

2. Regular. This setting agitates more for tougher clothes.

3. Delicate. This one has slower agitation and should be used with warm and cold water, not hot. This is the one for your favorite blouses, knits, washable silks and wools, lace-trimmed items, and less-sturdy stuff.

Most machines have temperature charts printed inside the lid or in the manufacturer's pamphlets. But this is a good guideline:

✴ White cottons, linens, and towels: Use a hot wash and a cold rinse.

✴ Colored cottons, jeans, towels, colored shirts: Use a warm wash and a cold rinse.

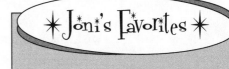

✴ Easy care, permanent press, wrinkle free, knits, and mixed loads: Use a warm wash and a cold rinse.

For delicates and fine washables that require a milder detergent, I like Woolite or Ivory.

✴ Delicates, fine washables, sweaters: Use a cold wash and a cold rinse.

✴ Rinsing in cold water will help prevent shrinkage.

Put the recommended amount of detergent into the washing machine, then set the heat level and cycle you prefer and let the water fill halfway to its maximum for your setting. *Now* the soap has mixed in enough, and you can add the clothes. Add them loosely. They will not get clean if you pack them in tightly, as clothes need room to swish around.

What happens if you add the detergent last? It may not mix in as well, and powder detergents may clump. If the detergent

✳ Joni's Favorites ✳

For regular laundry detergents, I like Tide and Wisk.

is not evenly distributed through the water, you won't get a consistently clean load.

If you want to add a liquid softener and your machine has a little dispenser, you can add it now and your machine will know when to release it. If you have no dispenser and still want to add softener, add it to the last rinse cycle. (Vinegar works well, too.)

Sweaters

Earlier I mentioned that I started hand washing my sweaters in college. But guess what—nearly all sweaters can be machine washed. Only occasionally do I find myself filling a sink and swishing a delicate sweater in cool, cautious suds. If you decide to hand wash, add a capful of creme rinse or glycerine when you rinse them, and they'll stay soft.

Most sweaters do fine on a delicate wash cycle, and some even withstand delicate drying. For sweaters you're worried about, purchase a footed screen made for drying hand washables, put it in the tub or garage, and spread out a sweater to drip dry on it. If a sweater is extremely expensive, made of cashmere, or made of pure virgin wool, I'd take it to the cleaner's. Most acrylic and man-made fibers are washable. If your sweater is a dark color, wash it alone the first time, in case the dye bleeds. And to see if you should chance it at all, just wet a small area such as the cuff, and let it dry to see how it does with water. The main secret in washing sweaters is to not put them in the dryer, where you'll risk shrinkage. (I once dried a wool sweater and it came out like a felt jacket for Barbie.) Let them air dry horizontally on a sweater rack.

Other drying methods are problematic: dryer heat may shrink the sweater, a towel doesn't work as well because there's no ventilation underneath, and a hanger allows the weight of the water in the sweater to pull it down and stretch it out.

Caring for Bedding

To care for linens—which includes sheets, pillowcases, towels, and blankets—simply treat them as separate loads of whites. Don't try to cram everything into one load. This is not a race. Wash the sheets alone. Then blankets alone (which also avoids getting blanket lint on other items). Then towels and washcloths. Sheets and towels should be done weekly, blankets only when soiled. Though if blankets are against your skin, they'll need to be washed as often as sheets.

You may be wondering why, if you shower every day, you have to wash sheets every week. After all, you're clean when you're in them, right? Not exactly. We all shed skin (scientists have examined common house dust and found that it is mostly made up of skin), we perspire, we drool (bless our hearts), we produce body oils, we sneeze, we exhale bacteria, our hair products and skin lotions rub off, and finally dust settles on sheets and attracts dust mites. If we have pets, sicknesses, allergies, or injuries, they only add to the problem. The dirt may not be as visible as a gravy stain on an apron, but to keep sheets truly fresh—and smelling fresh—they need frequent laundering in hot water. And don't forget to launder your mattress pad periodically, too.

Most pillows can be washed on a gentle cycle with warm water. Do two at once to balance the load, and add a clean tennis shoe when you put feather pillows in the dryer (it will help to fluff them). A squashed pillow can be fluffed on the air setting. Wash your pillows at least two or three times a year.

Some other items to wash once or twice a year are mattress pads, dust ruffles, decorative exterior shower curtains, and seldom-used blankets and throws. Upholstery and carpet cleaners can service your home yearly, and a good dry cleaner can take care of your draperies.

Frequency

So how often do you have to do laundry? In my house of four children and two adults, our machine runs every day. It seems that somebody is constantly washing something, either clothes or linens. But if you're on your own, once a week should suffice.

If you find you are blessed with so much underwear and so many clothes that you can go two or three weeks without laundering, you should still wash weekly because piling up dirty clothes creates unpleasant odors (and a huge washing task when you finally get to it).

Drying

When the clothes have finished spinning, place them in the dryer (one wash load is generally one dryer load). Again, don't pack your dryer too full or it will take all day to dry and place too much strain on your machine. I usually toss in a fabric softening sheet along with my wet laundry.

Now you need to choose a setting. Most dryers offer four:

1. Fluff—no heat, just fluffing and tumbling for pillows and bedding.

2. Knit or Delicate—low heat.

3. Permanent Press or Cotton Sturdy—high heat, usually with an automatic cool down.

4. Regular, timed cycles—you pick how many minutes you want the dryer to run, and clothes dry at high heat.

If you want to reduce wrinkling, remove clothes while they're still warm and smooth them out or hang them right up. If you let dry laundry sit in the dryer, wrinkles will "set" and you'll have more ironing to do. Make sure you know when the load will finish, and allow for folding and hanging time at that moment. If you have certain items you know you'll want to iron, remove them while they are still slightly damp.

> **Tip**
> If a dress is clinging due to static electricity, rub a fabric-softener sheet under it, or use hair spray on it.

Always clean the lint filter after every dryer load. Just pull out the screen and bunch up the lint (it will stick to itself). Some machines will do this for your automatically.

The Single Sock Dilemma

What about the infamous lost socks? Are they really secretly meeting in some laundromat basement, planning a takeover of the world? No. In fact, most of the time they are secretly folded up into contour sheets as a result of someone washing linens with clothing, then overlooking the one sock that stuck to a sheet due to static electricity. I've also heard the theory that when the water level rises in a washer, a floating sock tumbles over the edge and down into the side of the machine. But I don't buy this one because wet socks would start to smell. Wherever they go, it's a cinch you'll lose one sooner or later, and there are two basic strategies for coping.

1. Buy all the same kind of socks. Then they'll always match up, and the worst that will ever happen is that you'll have one unmatched sock.

2. Clip socks together with the various gadgets and devices made for this. Even a safety pin will work.

What if it's too late and you already have a small mountain of unmatched socks? Save them for other uses. They make great dusting mitts, or can be placed over furniture legs when moving furniture, so they won't scratch the floor. Large socks are good to slip over shoes when packing a suitcase, to keep shoe dirt from getting on your clothing. And finally, if you pour two pounds of uncooked rice into a clean sock, knot the neck, then microwave for two minutes, you'll have a wonderful heat pack for cold feet or sore muscles.

Ironing

This brings us to ironing. Actually, there are a few ways to get out of ironing entirely.

1. Be like Madonna, and throw clothes away after you wear them.

2. Send clothes out for laundering or dry cleaning. This can get expensive, but sometimes it's worth it. A starched white shirt, freshly back from the cleaners, is not such a bad investment.

3. When shopping, avoid cottons and linens, which require ironing; check all care labels to be sure you're buying permanent press.

4. As mentioned earlier, remove clothes from the dryer while they're still hot, and smooth out wrinkles by hand.

5. Shake out wet laundry before putting it in the dryer and you'll reduce wrinkling.

6. Let wrinkled clothes hang in the bathroom while you shower, and see if the steam helps the wrinkles to fall out.

7. Prevent wrinkling by using a cold rinse before the spin.

8. Wear wrinkly clothes on purpose. Adopt a more casual style and wear scrunchy, flowing skirts and muslin tops that look intentionally rumpled.

Otherwise, you have to iron, and in any case, it's a worthwhile skill to learn, even if you do it only rarely. Cloth napkins always need to be ironed, for example, and even if everything you own says permanent press, believe me, "permanent" should be in quotes. A skirt will get shoved too tightly in between two others and develop unintentional pleats, a shirt sleeve will get folded up and not folded back down again—you know the story. So here's how to do it right.

First of all, obey your iron's setting. Don't try to iron silk on the highest setting for cotton or linen. Most irons are labeled—or at least their directions explain that synthetics and delicate fabrics must be ironed on a lower number, or cooler setting, than heavy natural fibers. If in doubt, start cool and work your way up to warm and then hot.

Next, spray steam or even use a spray bottle of distilled water to get out deep wrinkles. If you slightly dampen clothes before you iron them, they'll iron faster and crisper. Women used to gather dry clothes from the clothesline, sprinkle them damp again (my mother had a porcelain figure the size of a Coke bottle, wearing a perforated hat, that would sprinkle water when she shook it), and then store the clothes for a few hours before ironing them. To retain any evaporating moisture, your great-grandmother probably put the clothes in a laundry basket or pillowcase, all piled together and equally damp.

Few of us have time for such quaint strategies today. That's okay. Just keep your spray bottle handy, and remember that distilled water won't leave mineral deposits behind. Another quick method is to tumble the clothes in the dryer with a wet towel or two until they reabsorb some moisture. You can also use a dampened pressing cloth—just a handkerchief or clean rag—that you place between the iron and your clothing to in-fuse your clothes with some moisture. Be sure not to do any of this if you're ironing a fabric that water spots!

Tip

If you've dampened a load of ironing and can't get to it, pop it in the freezer. That way, you keep mildew from forming.

And definitely use an ironing cloth, even a dry one, if you're working with a suit that will become shiny if ironed directly. A good idea for preserving the exterior finish of fabrics—even corduroy—is to iron the item inside out. That way, only the inside surface gets direct heat.

Make sure the surface of your iron is clean. To remove burned-on starch, iron salt on a sheet of waxed paper. (Put newspaper under the waxed paper so the wax won't melt into your ironing board cover.)

Position your ironing board in whatever way that's comfortable for you; there is no "right" way, though you'll want to face the ironing board with the small end where you feel comfortable pressing collars and sleeves. I'm right handed, and I like having the pointed end on my left; it's easier for me to reach across with my "good" hand. If ironing something lengthy, use the wide end so you can iron more surface before moving the clothing along.

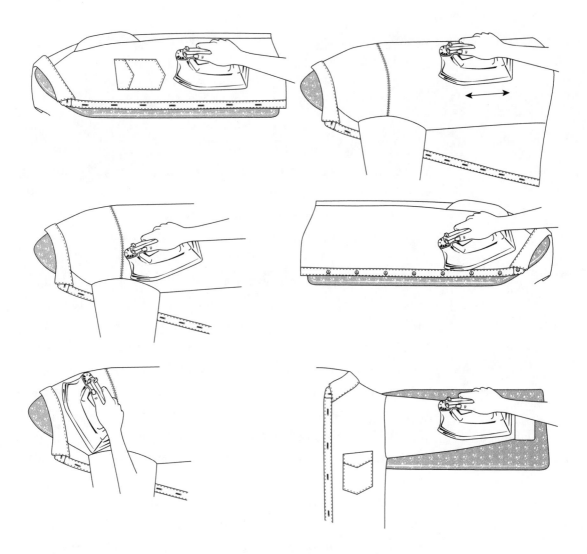

When you iron, go back and forth with the grain. Circular motions could stretch out your fabrics. And you don't need to push down hard on the iron; its heat and steam will do the job.

To iron a shirt, look at the way it was sewn—in pieces. Think of ironing each piece. First iron the front panel without the button holes; spray starch onto the shirt if you want a crisp finish. Now move the back panel into place, allowing the ironed

 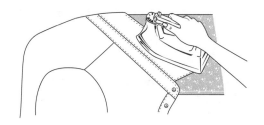

panel to hang down the front of the ironing board. Be sure to use the tip of the iron to get around the armholes. Now iron the front panel with the buttons. Move the iron in and around each button, but not over them (if your buttons are plastic, they could melt). Next, if there's a yoke or a top back panel, iron that. Now do the sleeves and cuffs. Turn them over and be sure you do each side. Last, press the collar, give it a fold crease, and give the shoulders a good crease. It takes some practice, but don't be daunted; after you've ironed your fair share of shirts, you'll become just as adept as your grandmother.

To iron pants, start with the waistband. Next, pull the pockets inside out and iron them. Then iron both sides of the pant legs, with seams aligned, and without putting the pockets into place just yet. This keeps ridges from forming around the pocket seams.

Never rest your iron with the hot side down. This may sound obvious, but it's a common mistake and will scorch your clothes or your ironing board cover. Always set your iron up, and when you're finished, allow it to cool before you put it away.

Unless you have bed linens that come out of the dryer wrinkle-free, I recommend ironing the pillowcases. It's so nice to lie down on a freshly pressed surface—and if you display your pillows, they'll look much more attractive in ironed

Listen to Your Mother!

Believe it or not, there is a right way to tuck in a shirt. My husband, who is a meticulous house-cleaning marvel himself, once was watching me stuff a T-shirt into my jeans and was amazed that I didn't know the right way to tuck in a shirt—T-shirt or otherwise. I was just stuffing its hem into the pants haphazardly, anywhere it stuck out. Oh, sure, I smoothed it down under the pants, but it puckered randomly around my waist. So if you are similarly out of the loop, pun intended, here's how to tuck in your shirt.

Shirts should have two pinch-pleats in front, one above each hip-bone, and two in back, below the shoulder blades. These pleats open toward your sides. Everywhere else it should be smooth and unwrinkled. This makes even more sense when you study a dress shirt or blouse, and you notice the two pleats under the yoke in the back. If you followed that line of vision downward, that's where the shirt would pleat to go into the pants. I was delighted to find this out, and cannot believe I lived twenty-some years without this information. What a difference—a properly tucked-in shirt looks much more polished and put-together.

But wait, there's more. There's even a right and a wrong way that your belt should point. You may have noticed that men's and women's blouses button on opposite sides, right? Well, the proper way to thread a belt around your waist is to follow that guide. If you're a woman, you start the belt on your left, so that it winds around your back, and comes forward on your right. This way the excess after you buckle it will point left and match the left-opening shirt lines of women's clothing. For men, it's just the opposite. And I thought I married my husband for his sense of humor.

pillowcases. Some time ago I bought some very expensive, high-thread-count sheets (680 count—and 350 is considered luxurious). I mentioned that they were so glorious I might just iron those as well. After all, people ironed sheets all the time in days gone by, right? Well, my husband just grinned and said he'd like to see me do it *twice*. He knew I'd do it once just out of ignorance (and finish the job out of stubbornness), but he also knew I'd resolve never to do *that* again! He was right. Sheets are unwieldy and cumbersome, and a pain in the patooty to iron! Now I remove the sheets from the dryer while they're still a bit damp, and I tug on them and snap them to pull the fabric tight, then I smooth out the wrinkles. If you're shopping for good sheets, get a thread count of at least 250, but also re-member that a little polyester blended with the cotton will keep them from wrinkling as much.

Mending

Everybody should know how to mend and sew on a button. It's plain foolishness to buy new clothes just because a hem or a seam has come loose. It only takes a few sec-onds to make most mending repairs, and we all have that kind of time as we talk on the phone, watch televi-sion, or wait for appointments.

Spray starch or hair spray will stiffen the end of a thread and make it easier to pass through a needle.

The trick is to have a mending tote. This can be a bag, a sewing box, whatever container you like, that is stocked with scissors, several spools of thread, and needles. When something needs mending, toss it into the tote for a later time when you can get to it. Then, as you're riding along in the back seat of a carpool, or talking to an old friend, your hands can be busy and you'll save wardrobe expenses.

There are some simpler ways to repair clothes short of threading a needle. In junior high I had a girlfriend who stapled her hems up when they came out. The Home Ec teacher nearly had a heart attack. Hey, at least my buddy didn't use duct tape. While I don't recommend stapling *or* duct tape, here are some other options.

1. There are fabric glues that are phenomenal for repairs. If a little braiding comes off a throw pillow, a rug unravels, or a curtain hem is drooping and I don't want to take the whole thing down, I reach for some fabric glue (there are many brands). It's like Super Glue for fabric. Don't use too much or it will look like a wet smudge soaking through the fabric. But a little can work a miracle.

   ✶ Joni's Favorites ✶

   For fabric glue, I prefer Fabri-Tac.

2. Fusible tape. This stuff is fabulous; you iron it between two surfaces, and it fuses them together. It comes in sheets or strips and works pretty well as long as you're careful when you launder and stick with cool temperatures. It's also good in a pinch if you plan to make a permanent repair later.

3. Adhesive Velcro dots. These are available at fabric stores and can hold something together for you until you can sew it.

4. The dry cleaners. They can make minor repairs for a price, and it may be worth it to you to salvage an expensive garment.

5. Marker pens. This isn't for repairing tears or seams, but for disguising dark clothes that got splattered with White-Out, paint, bleach, or any other permanent speck. Use a Sharpie—they come in black, purple, green, and red—and like a laundry pen, they won't wash out. Dab a dot of ink on that tiny white fleck and watch it vanish. My junior high girlfriend's Home Ec teacher would have a hernia, but she'll never know.

6. Revise the clothes. If the cuff of a shirt sleeve cannot be fixed, consider cutting off the cuffs and creating a short-sleeved shirt. Pants can be made into shorts, jackets can become vests, dresses can become skirts. Think before you toss!

Here's the right way to sew on a button. Thread a needle, double your thread and knot the end. (Use dental floss on white items; it lasts much longer than regular thread.) Hold the button where you want it, and come up from the bottom through one of the button's holes with your threaded needle. Now go down through the adjacent hole. Don't sew the button flush against the garment; leave enough room for the thickness of the fabric that has to button over it. Whether a two-hole or four-hole button, follow the same pattern of up through one hole and down through the other. Two or three loops per hole are plenty. Now, here's the part most people forget: wrap a shank around your threads, right beneath the button and above the fabric. Just wrap the remaining thread around and around the button threads, stitch it through the fabric, and knot it off on the underside. This will keep your button securely fastened for a long

> **Tip**
> Emergency button repair: Strip away paper from a storage bag twist-tie, and thread the wires through the button holes.

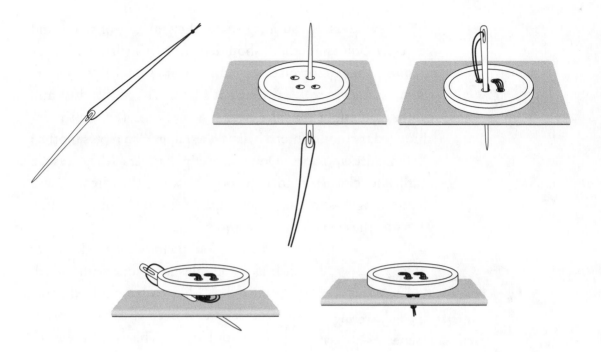

time. And here's a trick to keep the button on even longer: Dab clear nail polish over the threads on top of the button.

What should you do about clothes that tend to "pill," or form tiny balls? Knits are especially vulnerable, and I recommend de-pillers that "shave" them off and are made specifically for this purpose. If plain old lint is the problem, brush clothes while they're still damp *or* add a cup of vinegar to the final rinse of the wash. If lint or hair is the problem, you can use a lint roller, lint brush, loops of masking tape (sticky side out), or a rubber glove.

Storing Clothes and Linens

Once your clothes are washed, dried, ironed, and repaired, you need to store them properly. Here are the rules:

Fold sweaters. If you hang them, they fall out of shape and get little points in their shoulders from the hanger. Stack them on shelves, or place carefully in drawers. I like to store them on shelves so I can see what I have. To control dust and moths, you might consider clear sweater boxes. (For moths, include cedar chips or moth balls. Newspaper also repels moths.)

Hang dressy pants. Don't use clip hangers (they leave a mark and clothes tend to droop between the clips). Use a clamp hanger, and hang them upside down (from the cuffs). This way the creases will stay smoothest.

For casual pants, fold them over a thick hanger (such as wood, plastic, or one with a cardboard tube). I like to hang folded pants from a lower closet rod, usually beneath a rod for blouses. This is sufficient for jeans, khakis, and stretchy pants.

Tip

A quick clothes bag: Protect hanging garments from fading by covering with old pillow cases—just slip them over the hanger. This works especially well with leather and suede.

Hang skirts on clamps, and dresses on wood, plastic, or plastic-coated hangers. Don't cram them together; leave an inch between them. If you want to eliminate dust settling on the shoulders, cover with fabric garment bags or plastic shoulder shields—choose what works best for you. If you don't cover them, brush them frequently.

Hang all shirts, including T-shirts (they'll wrinkle less than if they're folded and stuffed into a drawer).

Hang jackets; do not use a coat rack or peg as it will pull jackets out of shape. Pegs are good for robes and nightgowns or belts and purses.

Store underwear in a dresser or chest of drawers, and use different drawers for different items. Drawer organizers and small containers are a great way to divide and conquer. Women, don't just throw all your bras, panties, and slips in one drawer; you'll run out of something and won't have advance warning. Keep all your bras together, all your panties folded in one place (if you die in a car wreck, somebody's going to have to go through these and you don't want to embarrass yourself, even if you are dead, so *fold* them) and so on. Keep trouser socks separate from pantyhose. Neat, clean living boosts morale, too.

Line shoes up on the floor, or—if you have a puppy—up high on shelves! You can also hang shoes in shoe pockets or keep them in a shoe closet or in clear boxes. Just don't kick them into a messy pile. By the way, a great trick for cleaning patent leather shoes or purses is to polish them with milk!

Organize your closet any way you like, but do organize it. Some people organize by work clothes and play clothes. Others by season. I like to arrange my clothes by color, in rainbow order. Depending where you live and what kinds of clothes you have, you'll know which method is best. But keep like things together, and you'll spend less time rummaging for what you need.

To store sheets, fold neatly and stack them in a linen closet. Flat sheets are easy to fold, but fitted ones can be exasperating. To make it easier: tuck one corner into the next, and so on, until all the corners are "pocketed." Then smooth and line up the sides, and fold as you would a top sheet. (See page 56.)

The right way to fold a towel is to fold it in thirds, lengthwise, then in half widthwise, and in half again. This looks tidy on the shelf, and then it hangs well over a towel rack when you're ready to use it.

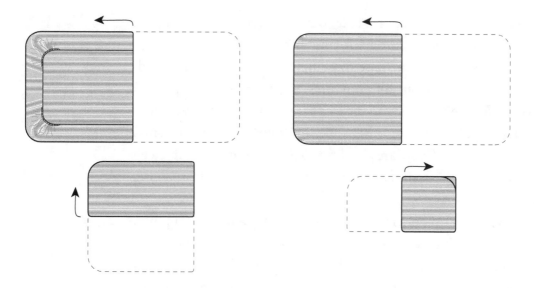

To keep sheets smelling fresh, make sure air can circulate. To prevent musty odors in sheets that aren't being used regularly, refold them on occasion. Also place an open box of baking soda or of activated charcoal in your linen closet; it will also help absorb odors and keep your sheets smelling fresh. Some people like to tuck in a scented sachet to give fragrance to their sheets and towels.

Packing a Suitcase

I wish I had a travel mile for every time I've packed a suitcase; I think I could circle the globe indefinitely. Here's how professional travelers pack a suitcase:

First, it really does make sense to travel light. Whenever possible, just use a soft-sided, rolling suitcase that will fit into the overhead compartment of an airplane. You can breeze right by baggage claim without having to wait, and you'll never have to worry about lost luggage.

Listen to Your Mother!

Some people roll their clothes before packing them, and claim this reduces the chance of wrinkling. Others overlap them, laying slacks halfway into the bag on one side, a skirt halfway in on the other, and so on, then folding the whole stack together when finished. Some place tissue paper between their clothes. I've tried all these methods, and I still go back to simply folding items and laying them neatly in the suitcase. I do make sure to fold pants just once at the knee, if possible, and I fold skirts in half vertically. What seems to make the most difference, though, is having the right size bag for your stuff; if it's too small, your clothes will crush tightly together. If it's too large, your belongings will tumble around. You need a bag that holds clothes gently but securely in place. Then fill the bag, but don't stuff it.

If you do need to check bags, make sure your name and address is on yours, and attach a bright tag or sticker so you can quickly identify yours from a look-alike.

Balance the contents of your bag. Heavy items, such as shoes or a cosmetics case, can be placed on opposite sides, so maneuvering with your bag will be easier. Always use shoe bags (or a large sock, as mentioned earlier) to protect your clothes from soil.

Pack items that tend not to wrinkle. Leave linen at home, unless you want to spend part of your vacation ironing. When shopping, you can scrunch the sleeve of a shirt with your hand to see if it retains wrinkles or not. I've had great luck with clothes made of synthetics, such as rayon or polyester blends.

To keep wrinkles on suits and dresses to a minimum, use a garment bag that allows them to hang freely.

Choose a color scheme for your trip, so you won't have to take multiple sets of shoes and purses to match each outfit; everything will go with navy, or black, or whatever you've chosen. This is one of the big secrets to traveling light—mixing and matching slacks, sweaters, and shirts and blouses that are all interchangeable. Women should take comfortable shoes that look great with pants *and* skirts.

Keep a checklist of everything you need, then you won't arrive without your slip, your razor, or other items commonly forgotten. And be sure to include a plastic trash bag for dirty clothes.

I always place pajamas in the suitcase last, so that I can get ready for bed without digging through my suitcase. And if I have items that must look pressed and fresh, I take time to hang those up as soon as I arrive.

When assembling your cosmetics case, use travel-size toothpaste and shampoo if you can, to reduce both the weight and bulk of your luggage. When my regular tube of toothpaste gets down to the last inch, I set it aside for travel—and I do the same with other items such as lotions and creams.

Air pressure can cause many containers to leak, so prevent a disaster by storing "leakables" in a Zip-Loc bag, where they can't spill on a hairbrush or your clothing. You can also reduce the chance of leakage by squeezing out as much air as possible and then screwing the cap on before you fly.

If you take medicine or vitamins, count out the right amount and take it along in a plastic film canister or a pill box, instead of packing giant bottles. To keep tablets from crumbling as they rattle around, tuck in a cotton ball or a tissue.

If packing for young children, use extra large Zip-Loc bags for each outfit. You just hand them a bag each morning, and you know they have clean clothes, fresh underwear, and matching socks. This also eliminates rummaging.

Chapter Five

Dusting

You want to make a billion dollars? Think of a way to keep dust out of people's houses and apartments. Nobody has yet conquered the infamous dust bunny, or discovered how to banish it once and for all. And until they do, we must take on the battle woman by woman and man by man.

Prevention First

The best way to deal with dust is to prevent it. You won't be able to create a completely dust-free environment, but you can take steps to greatly reduce how much accumulates.

Walking It In

Most dust and dirt comes into our homes from outside, and most of it on our shoes. Get a good, bristly doormat and use it. If you want to go a step (no pun intended) further, take your shoes off by the front door and make your home a stockings-only environment. Or pull a Mister Rogers and have a second set of clean shoes waiting for you to wear while you're inside. This is fine for family, but I also have a number of friends who post a "no shoes, please" sign in their entryway and ask visitors to remove their footwear before coming in. This may be met with mixed reactions, as many people are cold or uncomfortable without shoes—and after all, you want guests to feel welcome. You might keep a basket of booties for guests to slip over their shoes, but how sterile do you really need to be? And how many guests are traipsing through your house each day? Unless you're conducting tours of some kind and your carpet is getting worn down to nothing, I'd say relax the rules for friends. Maybe use a couple of throw rugs, and definitely consider traffic before you install white carpet.

> **Tip**
>
> According to experts, we breathe in two tablespoons of solid dust particles every day. And we each accumulate forty pounds of dust per year!

Filters

Another way to prevent dust is to check your heating and air-conditioning filters monthly, and replace them when dusty. For really clean air, make sure you have the (expensive but worth it) HEPA kind that block allergens. Having the right filter can cut down considerably on the time you spend dusting. Now check the filter on your vacuum—many actually "spray" dust back into your home.

Animals

Groom pets outdoors to eliminate as much shedding and dander as possible. Even a quick wipe-down with a damp paper towel will pick up hair that would otherwise settle on your furniture.

Disguising Dust

Choose furnishings that don't show every speck of dust. A rough, pale-painted finish instead of glossy, dark wood will appear less dusty, even if it isn't. We had a shiny cocktail table BK (before kids) made of beautiful hardwood. It worked perfectly in our family room. Over the years it got dinged and scratched by our growing family, and we painted it first a creamy yellow, then a shade of rose. Finally I realized it was going to look "distressed" no matter what, so I painted it navy blue, followed by a coat of white. Then I attacked it with a sander, removing much of the white, and giving it a kind of stone-washed blue jeans, casual effect. Now it looks great, goes with our new white-and-navy color scheme, and every foot that rests on it and chips off more paint just makes it look better.

Reduce Dust Catchers

Opt for hanging shades or blinds instead of curtains, which hold more dust and allergens.

Reduce the number of knickknacks, silk arrangements, and doo-dads we tend to accumulate; they all need dusting, and then must be moved so you can dust under them. You'll save a lot of work time if you choose a less cluttered decor—the more streamlined, the easier to keep clean. Spare decorating has a fluid elegance, too, and lets you emphasize your truly special pieces.

Tip: A great way to dust computer keyboards and other intricate items is to spray them with an automotive product—a can of pressurized air.

Keep plastic covers over your computer/electronic equipment. Invest in a tiny keyboard vacuum.

Sounds crazy, but consider leather furniture. Lots of folks swear by how easy it is to keep clean. They just wipe it down, and they never have to worry about ground-in dirt, fading, or the wear and tear on fabric. Spilled liquids don't soak in, and pet hair doesn't stick. Unless someone punctures a hole in it, it's probably the most durable choice.

If you're installing bookcases or shelves for display, consider cabinets with glass doors. You can still see what's on the shelves, but the doors will block a considerable amount of dust.

What Is Dust, Anyway?

This is kind of like asking, "How many germs are passed during a kiss?" It's information we don't always want to know. Nevertheless, knowing will probably convince you to dust regularly, so read on.

Insect parts—Cockroach and ant invasions aside, there will always be a fly, a gnat, a spider—*something* that gets into your domicile and meets its death there. Its dry old carcass soon crumbles apart, but, alas, it does not vanish or evaporate. It becomes part of your environment unless you sweep it up and toss it out. And if you do have an insect invasion, the problem multiplies.

Pollens, molds, fungus, spores—All those nose-tickling airborne particles blow in from outside (and thrive if your home is too damp).

Microorganisms and bacteria—They're everywhere, but especially in dust.

Animal dander and hair—Obviously, pets contribute greatly to dust, but so will unwanted rodents, who also "mark" their territory and leave excrement behind.

Smoke—Even if no one smokes in your home, you bring it in on your clothes from the world outside.

Food particles—Forgotten crumbs, splatters, flecks of salt, you name it. These also attract pests.

Flakes of skin—Unless you're secretly a reptile who sheds your skin once a year, you're going to lose flakes of skin and bits of hair on a regular basis.

Dirt—Airborne particles of soil and minerals from outside get blown about and some eventually find their way into your home.

Sawdust, plaster, and remodeling dust—Any house repairs that require clean-up can also contribute to your overall dust quotient.

Decomposing stuff—You know the musty smell of old books and clothes? They're deteriorating, and you're breathing in the molecules they're losing.

Tissue—Ever tuck a Kleenex into your purse or pocket and find it pulverized a few days later? Of course you have. Tissues are designed to break apart (especially toilet tissue), and using a lot of it releases minute paper particles that join the dust scheme.

Lint—Bits of fuzz and thread from fabric are inevitable, but at least they're usually large enough to see and pick up.

Powders and makeup—Wherever you get ready, you'll find a change in the dust—it will reflect the products you use to become beautiful. Just be sure to wipe them up so your home will stay beautiful, too.

Well, I hope you don't wake up screaming tonight. Knowing what's in dust is almost as scary as the videos that show, germ by germ, just how vile your counters and sinks are. If you watch *those*, you'll wear rubber gloves and an oxygen mask for the rest of your life. And we don't want that. So that's the last microscopic look we'll take at the world right under your nose. Just be sure to dust, okay?

Dusting 101

Now, even if you take all those steps, you're going to have to dust, and generally once a week. Dusting is the first thing you should do when you start cleaning your house, by the way, because we clean top to bottom and this way you won't knock dust or dirt onto freshly cleaned floors.

Begin like a pro: work your way around the room, in either a clockwise or counterclockwise order, so you don't waste time crisscrossing, and you don't overlook something.

First, straighten and put away. Gather everything that goes into the bedroom, for example, into one basket, bag, or pile. After you've cleared the room, then carry those items to the appropriate room and put them away. (This prevents wasted steps as you put away each item and then come back for another.)

The Right Rag

What should you use for dusting? Don't use paper towels or relatively new cloth towels; they'll leave lint and particles behind. Tear up old T-shirts and towels, or buy a package of cloth diapers. The best rags are old ones that have no lint left! Stop by a thrift store and look for old linen dish towels. Don't worry about stains; you're using these for cleaning rags, and they're some of the best.

Bunching up a rag into a ball is not the way to clean. Fold your rag in half, then in half again. This will give you eight cleaning surfaces to use: when one gets dirty, switch to a new rectangle, and finally turn the whole thing inside out. You'll use and launder fewer rags this way.

Start at the Top

First, check the top corners and light fixtures in your home. Use an extension pole or climb a ladder to remove any cobwebs. Use a rag and furniture polish to dust wooden fan blades and the tops of high furniture such as media centers, bookcases, and armoires. If you have plastic surfaces—such as mounted speakers or smoke alarms—use an all-purpose cleaner on those. For glass light fixtures and windows, use glass cleaner. Do you have tall plants? Wipe their leaves with a damp cloth. Dust molding, tops of door frames, and tops of doors. Silk plants can be placed in the shower for a quick rinse.

Tip A soft paint brush will dust miniblinds in a flash.

Use the brush attachment of your vacuum to tackle the tops of window treatments. Curtains and valances trap a lot of dirt, and every time they're opened or brushed against, some of the dust swirls into the air. Once a year, send draperies out for a thorough cleaning.

Dusting the Midrange

If you have miniblinds or shutters, the best trick is to put on cotton gloves, spray them with the appropriate cleaner, and wipe the blades down.

Lamp shades can also be cleaned with the brush attachment on your vacuum, or with a regular paint brush. Wipe the bulbs with a damp cloth. For picture frames and breakables, I use an ostrich feather duster or a blow dryer set on low, directing dust to the floor. If your pictures hang crooked, press a tiny dot of teacher's putty onto the backs of the corners, then onto the wall. They'll stay put.

Next, use the upholstery attachment to vacuum the fronts of your curtains and your furniture. Don't forget to clean behind cushions, and clean any throw pillows. Now set the vacuum aside, as you'll need it for the carpet in a few minutes. If there are spots on your upholstery, test an inconspicuous area before you spot clean. There are terrific upholstery cleaning products on the market, but sometimes a dab of shaving cream will do the trick.

Spray or apply dusting wax to your rag, rather than spraying it right onto wood furniture, where it can accumulate in crevices, drip down legs, or overspray onto the rug. Now polish the wood in circular motions, so you won't get streaks. Don't polish around a book or lamp; move it and polish underneath, then replace the object. If you have white rings on wood furniture, rub plain white toothpaste into the mark, then wipe it off with a moist towel. (Add baking soda if the white marks are especially stubborn.) If there are small nicks or imperfections in your pieces, try the crayons and markers available for concealing wood scratches; they come in oak, walnut, and so on. Most hardware stores have them. Or rub a piece of that wood's nut right into the scratch, such as the meat of a walnut on walnut wood.

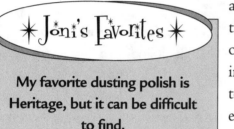

Joni's Favorites

My favorite dusting polish is Heritage, but it can be difficult to find.

If you find paper stuck to wood surfaces, soak it with salad oil until it slips off. Stickers can be removed with vinegar.

Don't use dusting wax on vinyl; only use soap and water.

Dusting Glass

Now look around the room for glass—have you missed any mirrors, windows, vases, or glass-covered pictures? If you have tough spots on windows, for example, try full-strength vinegar on them. Lots of people swear by newspaper for wiping a window really clean. But professionals use a squeegee, and I find that's the best (also newspaper ink could stain your windowsills). Believe it or not, you can conceal small scratches in glass with toothpaste. For wiping down TV and computer screens, only use a very lightly water-moistened cloth, as cleaners could damage them (see also chapter 9, "Cleaning for Sparkle and Shine").

I always check the walls, doorways, light switches, and doorknobs at this point. I use all-purpose cleaner and remove any fingerprints or marks that have accumulated. You can also use a sponge and soapy water.

From Top to Bottom

Last, look down at the baseboards and the hearth, if you have one. Brush or wipe them clean, and you're all done. Just toss the dirty rags and brushes into the washing machine, and you're ready to vacuum—the last step! (See chapter 7 for a discussion of floor care.)

Chapter Six

Caring for Finer Things

✳

Most of us possess at least a few fine things or family heirlooms—whether a crystal bowl that was a present from Mom, an antique dresser from grandparents, or a complete set of china and silver from our wedding. In addition, as we furnish our homes, it makes sense to buy high-quality items that will last a lifetime; when purchasing furniture, artwork, and even pots and pans, we often choose well-made products that we can pass on to our own kids someday. In short, over the years we accumulate a variety of treasures and beautiful objects that require special handling and care, and this chapter discusses how to make them last.

Candlesticks—To remove wax from candlesticks, freeze them and then break off the wax. Or heat the wax with hot water or the hot air of a blow dryer until it melts, then wipe it away. (By the way, I always freeze my candles before using them; it makes them last longer and drip less. Also, never display candles with unburned wicks; it's an age-old sign of hospitality if the wick has already been burned.)

Chandeliers—Place a drop cloth beneath the fixture and underneath your ladder, if you'll need to climb. Hold a container of glass cleaner up so that the crystals are immersed in it for a second or two; let them drip dry. Or use the same method as for cleaning blinds—wipe the crystals with cleaner-soaked cotton gloves.

China—Store with flannel plate separators between each dish, to prevent chipping. Thin cardboard, paper towels, or paper plates also work. Wash and dry china by hand, especially if it has gold or silver rims. If china is stained, denture-cleaning tablets may help.

> **Tip**
> For cut glass and cut crystal, use liquid (not granule) Cascade dishwasher soap.

Copper and brass—Both of these metals clean up with vinegar-based solutions, even ketchup! Leave it on a few minutes, then wipe away the tarnish.

Crystal—Avoid extreme temperatures and abrasion with crystal: hand wash using a soft cloth and line your sink with either a towel, a rubber mat, or a dishwashing pan to prevent breakage if a piece should slip from your hands.

Hardwood floors—Sweep or dry mop most of the time, and occasionally damp mop with any of several products made just for cleaning wood. To prevent squeaking, rub talcum powder into the cracks.

Jewelry—I like commercial jewelry cleaners that come in a plastic tub with a little basket inside to hold your baubles. But glass cleaner or toothpaste also work.

Leather upholstery—Clean with saddle soap. Prevent cracks by rubbing with a solution of 1 cup linseed oil and ½ cup vinegar.

Marble surfaces—Spills of various kinds, and oils from our skin, can discolor marble (and for this reason never use oily products on it). Wash it with a nonabrasive cleaner such as SoftScrub. There's also a great product on the market called Marble Magic. Or rub with a paste of water and baking soda. Some experts recommend a light polish with salt and lemon, but I find that salt can scratch delicate surfaces. Sunlight is also a good whitener.

> **Tip** Alka-Seltzer can polish jewelry, toilet bowls, vases, and Thermos bottles.

Pewter—Usually soap and hot water are all you need, but occasionally, to bring out the luster of an antique piece, buff it with silver polish. To keep it in good condition, avoid contact with acids.

Pianos—Dust the wood as you would any fine piece of furniture. Keep keys clean by washing your hands before you play, and by occasionally wiping the keys with toothpaste and a dampened cloth, then a dry cloth to buff.

> **Tip** Shine pewter with a cabbage leaf.

Porcelain—Dab with salt and lemon juice, or with diluted bleach (test first).

Rock or brickwork—Stains from smoke, barbecues, and fireplaces leave a grimy appearance. Tackle them with an art gum eraser.

Rugs—Vacuum frequently to prevent the wear caused by dust and sandy particles. If storing, wrap in newspaper to discourage moths.

Silver—There are many varieties of silver polish. Just spray it on and wipe it off. If you're out of silver polish, toothpaste will work in a pinch. And always dry silver thoroughly; don't let it air-dry. There are two ways to prevent tarnish in the first place: Use your silver regularly and hand wash it, or keep it from exposure to air, and thus oxidation, by wrapping it securely in a flannel cloth meant to prevent silver tarnishing.

✳ Joni's Favorites ✳

I like Hagerty Silversmith's spray for polishing silver; it's the simplest and seems to last the longest.

Suede—Rub with ground, uncooked oatmeal, then brush off.

Tablecloths—To store, do not fold them and stuff them in a drawer; fold them loosely and hang them over a thick hanger in the closet. Occasionally change how they're folded to prevent creasing and discoloration. Always leave a crease down the center, however, as this is a good way to make sure your cloth is centered on the table (and it's an acceptable crease to leave in when entertaining). Remove spots quickly (see the stain removal guide in chapter 4), launder and iron.

Tip

Never allow rubber items, such as rubber bands, to come in contact with silver; rubber will make silver tarnish.

Vases—Toilet bowl cleaner or denture cleaning tablets are both great for dissolving the scum that builds up inside vases—just add water and wait.

Velvet—Don't use water or you'll ruin velvet. Try a light brushing of dry-cleaning solvent.

Wedding gown—Have it hermetically sealed in a box, by a dry-cleaning shop, to make sure air won't destroy this heirloom. The box should have a plastic window so that you can see you have the right dress when you pick it up.

Wedding bouquet—Place in a bucket or container large enough to hold the arrangement. Carefully sprinkle silica gel crystals around the blossoms to dry and preserve the flowers. After the bouquet has dried, display it under a glass dome, or behind glass doors. You can also make your own drying powder by mixing 10 parts cornmeal with 3 parts borax.

Listen to Your Mother!

You need to insure your valuables. Whether you own a home or a condominium, or you're renting an apartment, you need insurance.

First, take pictures of any items of value that you'd want replaced in the event of a theft, flood, or fire. You might also do a video tour of your entire home, showing the valuables. Keep the pictures or video in a fireproof safe, at a relative's home, or in a safe deposit box at the bank. I had a friend who was sure a small metal safe would protect his belongings, but he didn't bolt it down and the burglars stole the safe! Another great place to store important documents is in the freezer; it survives most fires.

Be sure your property is labeled with serial numbers, if applicable. Some people buy electric engravers and write their names on items that have no other identification.

Keep receipts to document the value of your belongings. If some items are extremely valuable, have them appraised professionally.

Most of your personal property should be covered in your homeowner's policy; carefully research and talk with several agents to educate yourself and to make sure you're getting the most coverage you can for what you can afford. Make sure popular theft items are covered: jewelry, silver, electronic equipment, music systems, antiques, artwork, and so on. Realize that the more insurance you want, the higher the premium you'll have to pay. If you only want your property covered for the (used) value it had when it was stolen, that will cost a lot less than if you get replacement-cost insurance, which will replace the item new.

Wicker—I recommend new homeowners furnish their first living room with high-quality patio furniture, such as wicker. Then, when you can afford what you really want inside, move the wicker outside. This makes more sense than investing hundreds of dollars in mediocre furniture that you're going to have to give away at some point, or someday sell in a garage sale for fifty bucks. (And you'll still have to buy patio furniture.) To care for wicker, wash it with warm salt water, then apply lemon oil monthly. Don't let it freeze or get too dry.

Watches, gold—Let a jeweler service and clean your watch periodically. To keep a link-style gold band from wearing out, keep it scrupulously clean (gold is so soft that grime and dirt wear it away between the joints).

Woodwork or wood furniture—Some solutions are discussed in chapter 5, but if you're working with water marks on an old antique and it doesn't respond to toothpaste or baking soda, try a paste made of lemon oil and rottenstone (from the hardware store). Remember to rub with the grain.

Chapter Seven

Floor and Carpet Care

1 once had a small area rug that I wanted cleaned, but I was too cheap to hire professionals. So I got the idea that my teenage son and his friend could throw it across the top of the car and shampoo it at one of those do-it-yourself car washes. What would that cost at the most—three dollars? Needless to say, they were amazed at the amount of dirt that came out of the rug when they sprayed it with those power nozzle wands. And you know what? It came clean! I wouldn't recommend this very often, as harsh detergents could be just as bad for a valuable rug as the dirt and dust are. But sometimes it pays to think outside the box, as they say.

An Ounce of Prevention

The best way to take care of floors and carpets is by keeping them clean in the first place. If you looked at dirt and grit under a microscope (I know, I promised no more microscopes, but bear with me), you'd be amazed at how sharp it is. Those

77

jagged edges cut carpet fibers and scratch hard floors. Let's go back to a car example—if your car is dusty, you want to rinse it off, not brush it and scratch the finish, right? Well, your carpet—and floor—will last longer and look newer the more often you vacuum it to remove those sharp particles.

What—vacuum a hard floor? Yep, whenever possible. The strong suction will pick up much more dirt than your broom will. But let's talk about carpets first.

Lots of people like to go barefoot, and far be it from me to talk you out of this if you are one of them. But . . . this is how foot fungus spreads. At least promise to wear slippers in hotel rooms, where you have no idea who's been walking barefoot on those carpets before you. I prefer to wear socks, slippers, or shoes even at home, and I'm probably keeping my feet, and my carpets, cleaner by doing so.

Warm or Cold?

Let's also look at the warmth factor of floors. If you have bare floors and bare feet, you're going to be colder than if you have carpet or socks for insulation. Tile will feel colder than wood, and marble will feel still colder than tile. Why is this? Isn't everything in your home the same temperature? Of course it is—you don't have 72-degree walls and curtains and 52-degree floors. The reason floors feel cold under our feet is because of conduction. Fabric is a lousy conductor, so carpeting doesn't draw much heat away from our feet. But put your foot on tile or stone, and it will immediately conduct warmth away from your skin and make it feel colder. Cold floors are a tactile illusion, if you will. So keep warm, for your mother, and wear a pair of socks.

Always empty vacuum bags outside, so you don't refill your house with dust.

Vacuuming and Carpet Care

Before you vacuum, pick up all the tiny stuff that's visible to the eye. If you hear pins and pennies clicking through your vacuum hose, you're asking for a jammed machine at some point. Brush the edges of the carpet by the walls, to loosen dust and bring it away from the wall to where the vacuum can get it. I use a toothbrush for this. If you skip this step, it won't be long before the edges of your carpet look black. (And no, you shouldn't buy black carpet thinking to get away with this—dark rugs show every speck of lint. Besides, you want your environment to *be* clean, not just look clean.)

Tip

Lose an earring or a contact lens? Pull a nylon stocking over your vacuum hose and vacuum the area. The stocking will keep the small item from going down the hose.

Now hold the vacuum handle in your "good" hand, and the cord in your other. Go over the rug in neat, adjacent rows. Not only does this look best when you're finished, but it's the way to insure a thorough job. Use an extension cord when you vacuum, so you won't have to keep plugging and unplugging the cord as you move along.

Move furniture entirely out of the way when you vacuum, then replace it. If your furniture is hard to slide, put it on a throw rug and then pull the rug. To prevent indentations from sofa legs, use plastic coasters under them. (I'm assuming you've already vacuumed the upholstered furniture and pillows when you were dusting, as outlined in chapter 5.)

If you have carpet dents you want to get rid of, spray them lightly with water to hasten the "scrunching" of the pile, then let it dry without any furniture on top. Hot water and a blow dryer are the answer for stretched-out wall-to-wall carpeting that bubbles. Simply dampen the carpet and heat it to make it shrink. Just be sure not to use too much water on a carpet; you'll risk mildew.

Extra Help

For professional carpet cleaning, I prefer the dry methods. But if you do moisten a carpet to clean it, don't put furniture back until it's completely dry. For one thing, the dust and dirt on your shoes will form mud, and for another, anything metal will make rust marks. You can rent commercial carpet cleaners from certain grocers, party rental companies, and such. Check the yellow pages.

For cleaning narrow nooks and corners, use the narrowest vacuum attachment you can, or the hose by itself. A hand-held minivacuum also helps in these instances.

Removing Spots

A burn or a surface stain on carpeting can sometimes be rubbed away with fine sandpaper. If a mark is hopeless, however, replace it with a plug of the same carpet (always save some when carpet is initially installed, or ask your landlord if he or she saved any). I've had to do this several times, and it's a great solution.

When anything spills on your carpet, wipe it up as quickly as possible with paper towels. Work from outside of the spot toward the center to keep from spreading the stain. After you blot up all that you can, use a spot remover or carpet cleaner of your choice. For really stubborn stains, try shaving cream or a dab of laundry detergent. To blot up all the moisture when you're finished, step (or stomp) on paper towels until they won't absorb any more liquid.

Tip You can "dry clean" your carpet by sprinkling it with cornstarch, then vacuuming.

What happens when you spot-clean and lift out more than the stain? Some cleaners are too strong and will remove your carpet's color, so you should always test them first in an inconspicuous area. Even so, if you have a lightened or sun-bleached spot on your carpet, you can dab on permanent marker in the same color as your carpet—artist's supply stores have every shade imaginable. Food coloring and Rit Dye can also be sponged on carefully. After your color has dried, dab it with diluted vinegar so the color will stay.

To remove candle wax from carpet, iron the spot with a paper sack between the iron and the carpet until all the wax has been absorbed by the paper. Chewing gum can be frozen with an ice cube, then removed.

Fruit stains will come out with repeated applications of salt, vacuuming between applications.

Grease splatters should be treated with talcum powder, baking soda, or cornstarch to absorb the oil. When dry, vacuum up the powder.

Plants can leave terrible carpet stains, as moisture soaks through clay pots and into your rug. Be sure to use plant stands or stick-on corks to elevate the pot and allow air to circulate underneath.

Fido, No!

Pet stains are a nightmare, especially cat urine, as it is so much more concentrated than dog urine. If it has soaked through to the carpet pad, you'll have to replace the carpet and pad to insure that your cat will not revisit the area. I once moved into a home that had allowed cats to use the carpeted dining room as a litter box. It wasn't until I pulled up the carpet, pad, and some of the flooring, then covered it with marble tiles, that the odor was gone. However, such extreme steps are not usually necessary. There are wonderful products on the market that neutralize the odor, and after you clean up as best you can with vinegar and carpet cleaner, apply one of these and cross your fingers.

✳ Joni's Favorites ✳

Nature's Miracle, Folex, and Chem Dry Stain Extinguisher are some of my preferred carpet cleaners.

Padding

Area rugs should have rug pads under them, not only so they'll be more comfortable to walk on, but to protect carpet threads that would otherwise rub against a hard floor. The right pad can also prevent a rug from slipping out from under you. To prevent tripping, cut your pad an inch smaller than the rug on all sides, so the rug can "flow" over the pad and stay flat on the floor. There are also products you can paint or spray on the underside of a rug to keep it from slipping.

If you're having carpet installed, choose a cushy rug pad, not the very cheapest one. I like to double-pad my carpets for extra softness, but if you've chosen a loose-weave carpet, a thick pad will accentuate bends on stairways where the fibers separate and look sparse.

Hardwood and Vinyl Floors

Wood and vinyl floors will stay shiny longer if you take a couple of precautions. First, don't let furniture scrape over these surfaces. Dining tables can be placed on area rugs, or at the very least, chair legs can be fitted with plastic or felt pads that make scooting less abrasive. These pads can be the adhesive or nail-in kind; both are available at the hardware store.

Next, lift—don't slide—items across a hard floor. If some pieces are too heavy to lift, lug them on a blanket. Or, if the item has legs, put a sock on each leg so it won't scratch the floor.

Kick off high heels before walking on scratchable flooring, and if you do find black heel marks, try a pencil eraser, an art gum eraser, kerosene, or turpentine to get rid of them.

Tar is one of the stickiest problems you can have, but it will come off the floor if you rub it with paste wax. Crayon will come off vinyl flooring with silver polish.

✳ Joni's Favorites ✳

For wood floors, my favorite cleaner is Murphy's Oil Soap.

At our house, we have a pound pup we adore, and every time he hears the wind blow he goes barking and sliding across our hardwood floor, nails gouging all the way—even if I keep them trimmed. This inevitably means there

Listen to Your Mother!

Sometimes you find a great place to live, but the floor is damaged beyond repair. There are some creative ways to deal with this.

Here are my top ten ways to disguise an unattractive floor:

1. Consider strategically placed area rugs. They also reduce noise, add cozy comfort, and lend a decorator's touch to your room.

2. Lay out exercise mats and pretend you're always working out.

3. Wall-to-wall carpeting is more affordable if you ask carpet dealers for remnants and scraps—they'll probably have some large enough to fit your room and at a greatly reduced price. You can't always choose a custom color, but if you can find a big enough carpet ware-house, the selection will be larger than you think.

4. Paint the floor entirely. With any paint or stain, you'll need to clean and possibly sand the floor first, so it will "grab" the paint. Choose a dramatic color or a neutral; whichever suits you best—and remember, it's easy and cheap to change paint colors. To prevent the paint from wear and tear, use outdoor or boat paint, and seal it with several coats of varnish.

5. Stencil or paint an actual rug design on the floor. Add knots and fringe with an artist's brush and short, whisking motions. Craft shops have numerous designs and even stamp pads and rubber rollers to help you. Again, seal with varnish. Be

are scratches on the wood and our floor no longer shines like it did when it was new. But a piano finish on a floor is not practical if you have many kids or pets, so we've opted for a tail-wagging member of the family over a glossy shine you can see your face in.

brave. Be gutsy. You'll get a thousand compliments.

6. Splatter or sponge-paint your floor for high drama. (Use a new toilet brush to fling the splatter paint.) Set up an easel and it will look like an artist's studio. We once allowed one of our sons to splatter paint his entire bedroom and to paint the floor black. It looked jazzy and contemporary.

7. Consider adhesive "tiles" made of linoleum. You can buy boxes of these at the hardware store, usually twelve inches square, and in a variety of colors and designs. They're easy to install yourself; just follow the peel-and-stick instructions.

8. Decoupage can look very artsy—if you're at all creative, pick a theme (Modern, Victo-rian, Art Deco, Country, maybe a hobby or interest of yours) and gather pictures or posters of items you like. Cut them out and use Modge Podge to stick them onto your floor, then seal with multiple coats of varnish. Always let each coat dry before applying the next one.

9. If you can afford it, install a new floor of tile, brick, or wood. This will probably require the services of a professional, but you'll undoubtedly love the results.

10. Look into faux painting. Craft and paint stores can supply all you need to make your floor look like marble, granite, a stone walkway, blocks of wood, moss, even fabric. Think out-side the box!

Still, to keep your floors as shiny as possible, keep them clean. A light damp-mopping will pick up a lot of dust, but you can't rely on water alone to really clean your floors and re-move grease. Use one of the liquid cleaning products available at the supermarket. Some carpet dealers also sell excellent wood floor cleaning products. None of these should contain strong or abrasive chemicals, which can dull the wood's shine.

If you do plan to use water on a wood floor, only *lightly* damp mop, and be careful not to soak the floor—water can badly damage wood.

What about waxing? If your wood has a shiny urethane coating, it won't need waxing. But older, natural floors will need waxing, and the easiest way to apply this is with an electric buffer. Do *not* reach for the dusting wax, thinking that if it works on wood furniture, it must work on wood floors. It doesn't. It makes floors far too slippery, and as my mother would say, you'll fall and put your eye out.

Mopping

Older homes often have floors with wax build-up. Mop it off with a mixture of 1 gallon water and 1 cup ammonia. Incidentally, the right way to wet mop is the way sailors swab the decks: Immerse the mop in a bucket of cleaner, lift it out, and wring it over the bucket. Now twirl it so the mop strands flare in a circle. Place it quickly on the floor, splayed out. Do not mop up and back, as this is hard on your back—go side to side, and walk backward, erasing your footsteps as you go. For a dazzling shine on large floor surfaces, consider renting or buying a buffer. You can't possible generate enough elbow grease to compete with the shine of this whirling wonder.

Tip: If using a wet mop, use two buckets—one for wringing out the mop as it gets dirty, and a "clean" one for dipping the mop into fresh, soapy water or cleaning solution.

Chapter Eight

Pets

I'm a major pet lover. I love all kinds, and encourage people to have doting animals on which they can lavish affection and who will return that love to them. There really is something to the notion that pets improve your mental health. But they can also impact your physical health in negative ways, and that's what we're going to discuss here.

Members of the Family

Some time ago my husband went on a business trip and returned to find the dog (formerly banned from the kitchen) now circling through it like a shark, just waiting for a crumb to fall. Standards for the cat had also been relaxed while my husband was away; one was sleeping on the back of a sofa, another was curled up on a bed pillow. "You know," Bob said to me, setting down his suitcase, "If I hadn't married you—" And now I'm thinking he's been missing the heck out of me and he's going to say something romantic about how his life would have been incomplete, but instead he says, "—you would've been one of those women with forty cats."

It's true. I love my furry babies, and I don't maintain the rules when the cat's away, so to speak. I would let my dog lick my ice cream cone if I didn't think word would get out.

But in order to maintain household order and cleanliness, we need to be more like Bob and remember that animals are not people (well, not exactly), and there need to be some ground rules.

Should You Even Get a Pet?

If you don't already own a pet, think carefully before getting one. First, realize that most pets can be expensive to keep, especially cats and dogs. Pets require vaccines, vet visits, flea treatments, nail clipping, teeth cleaning, food, and sometimes additional expenses such as carpet cleaning, grooming, fencing, boarding, and training fees. I have discovered that there is no limit to the amount of money that can be spent on an animal. You could put three kids through college.

Next, consider whether the pet you want is compatible with your lifestyle. No big dogs in tiny apartments, no shedders if you can't stand animal hair, no cats in homes with allergic family members, no high-maintenance critters if you're too busy. Don't choose a dog for companionship, then fail to be a companion; he'll bark and howl in loneliness while you're at work all day. Get a hamster or a goldfish—a pet who's more independent and requires less maintenance.

Before you buy, make sure to learn what your pet will require in the way of housebreaking, feeding, exercise, and clean-up. Can you really do it?

And finally, double-check the rules of your apartment complex or neighborhood. Especially if you're considering a potbellied pig or a pygmy goat, check the zoning laws for farm animals. But even if you're legally allowed to have a gaggle of geese in your backyard, how will this impact your neighbors? Avoid pets that are guaranteed to disrupt the general welfare.

Even if your living situation is less than ideal, if you're a pet lover, like me, you will no doubt give in and get a furry companion anyway. If so, consider rescuing one from the pound. There are zillions of extra cats and dogs in the world—okay,

Listen to Your Mother!

Establish a routine your pet can expect. Feed twice a day, and keep water fresh. Place feeding dishes where you won't trip over them, and where spills won't create a problem. A bathroom or laundry room is usually best. If you choose a garage or an outdoor patio, you may have to contend with ants, mice, raccoons, and visiting pets from other households.

Every week, rinse the water dish and disinfect to remove slime and scum. I use a diluted spray of bleach, then rinse.

Clean up on a regular basis, too. Most cities have laws that dogs must be leashed, and their droppings must be picked up by the owner. Dispose of them every day in a sack, tie it, and place it in an outdoor garbage can. If your dog is using a surface other than dirt or grass (such as cement), disinfect it and hose it down weekly. If you keep up, you won't have the flies or odors associated with neglected droppings, nor will your animals track feces into your home on their feet.

maybe not zillions, but certainly a huge surplus—and it's good to rescue one that might otherwise be killed.

Then, neuter your pet. Unless you're going to show or breed your animal, this is the way to control the sadness of cat and dog overpopulation and the resultant need for their extermination.

Bringing Home a Puppy

There are few joys finer than bringing home a soft-furred, month-old, tail-wagging pup. However, this joy is often mitigated within a few hours (or minutes) when Spot needs to urinate for the first time—and does so where he stands. Your first chore, and it begins immediately, is to housebreak your dog. I've done this countless times, and there's only one way to do it. You have to take a week off. If you can't take a week off, buy lots of carpet cleaner and learn to swear.

Now, for one week, you follow that mutt everywhere he goes, and watch him like a hawk. If he even looks like he's thinking of squatting in your house, scoop him up and take him outside. Give him no opportunity to relieve himself inside. After he drinks or eats, take him out. In fact, take him out every hour or so, and lavish praise when he goes potty in the right place. If you turn your back for a minute, and he has an accident inside, do not hit him. Say "No!" firmly, and plunk him back outside. Going potty outside will earn your approval; going potty inside will not. A doggie door makes it easier for your animal to exit when he feels he needs to, but you can also get your dog to wait by the door, or whine, to let you know it's time. If you are diligent, your week will pay off and your dog will be permanently trained.

Some people train their dogs to go on newspaper. I fail to see how this is much better than going on the floor; you still have to clean it up, you still have to deal with what soaks through, and you still have the smell in your living quarters. What's more, heaven help you if you leave a newspaper lying on the sofa.

Some people like to crate their dog so that he won't go potty near his food dish. This works; he will whine for you to let him out, but once you're through crating him and he has run of the house, you'll still have to teach him not to go in the house.

Breaking Bad Habits

How do you get a dog not to chew up shoes and furniture? You supply him with plenty of approved alternatives. Puppies, and some dogs, simply need to chew. You shouldn't try to interfere with this basic need. Rather, you need to teach him what's okay to chew and what's not. So give him tasty chew bones, and whenever he's sniffing a leather shoe or a stuffed toy, firmly remove it and say, "No!" Then quickly give him what is okay—his own chewie. You can do this during Housebreaking Week.

Tip

If you want to give your dog rubber squeak toys and such, you can save money by purchasing a bag of used baby toys from a thrift shop for a dollar—instead of shelling out six or ten dollars in a pet shop for a toy that's just going to get chewed up.

If you let a dog chew on an old sock or shoe, he will think all socks and shoes are fair game. Make sure his chew toys are distinct from your belongings.

To keep your dog away from furniture, spray your furniture with Bitter Apple, a product made to taste nasty to dogs. On the other hand, is there such a thing as something that tastes nasty to dogs? I mean, they'll eat cat doo, right? I had a dog who loved Bitter Apple and licked it off thoroughly before going back to chewing on the furniture legs. But I have friends who swear by it.

Which reminds me. A dog trainer once told me that you can keep a dog out of certain areas by popping balloons (which will scare the dog) and then hanging the balloons on fences, and so on, where you don't want the dog to go. The dog will stay afraid of the popped balloon. Well, I tried it and my dog went berserk—happily berserk. She loved popping balloons and would push them around with her nose until she could corner one and burst it. Greatest toy she ever had. So much for the scary balloon method.

Another common complaint is that dogs jump up on people. You don't want this happening to your guests, even if you don't mind if she does it to you. So you need a consistent rule: No jumping on people. This is easy to cure. First, never slap your chest as if encouraging her to jump up. And don't let guests do it, either. When she jumps, just bend your knee to catch her in the chest (not hard, just enough to knock her down again). She'll soon stop.

Bringing Home a Kitty

How do you housebreak a cat? This is much easier than training a dog. With some cats, all you need to do is put them in the litter box and they get the idea. With others, you'll need to gather some feces, put those in the box, and let them make the scent connection that this is where the bathroom is.

Still, you'll have to clean a litter box, and I prefer to let my cats in and out at their leisure, going potty in the great outdoors. Cats are meticulous groomers, and will catch on quickly.

But what if your cat chooses another spot in your home for a litter box? Big trouble. See chapter 7 for one solution. Another is to confine your cat to a space just large enough for a litter box and her food, keeping them reasonably apart as cats don't like to defecate where they eat. After she gets the idea that she must use the litter box, gradually expand her space.

Some pet owners claim that ammonia is a great way to eliminate cat odors and prevent pets from returning to the scene of the crime.

And that brings us to another plan—start feeding her in the place where she used to potty (after you have cleaned and deodorized it as best you can). Sometimes this will break a bad habit.

Joni's Favorites

We like to use the antibacterial hospital disinfectant Odo-Ban to eliminate odors and clean an area that pets have dirtied.

Some cats spray to mark their territory. This is particularly true if you have more than one cat and they're trying to establish dominance. The best thing I've found is a hormone spray sold by veterinarians, which you apply to likely areas and which confuses the cat and makes it think it's already marked there. The spray is expensive but worth every penny.

Cats are notorious jumpers, and even if you train them not to jump on the kitchen counters, they're going to sneak and do it while you're away (you can trust your cat about as much as Eddie Haskell from *Leave It to Beaver*). But to train them as best you can, get a squirt bottle of water and spray them every time they jump onto a table or counter. They'll learn in a hurry, and they'll even still love you.

Other Pets

There are other pets that require far less care than a cat or dog (and some which, in my opinion, require more, such as horses and birds with all the clean-up). But if you're looking for other possibilities, do extensive research before you buy. A cool-looking snake doesn't look that cool when it's devouring a mouse. Some reptiles (skinks are a good choice) are very low-maintenance and easy to keep. Some eat mostly vegetation, others crickets. Inquire at the pet store about feeding and clean-up needs before you buy any pet, no matter how adorable it is. I'd also consider the life span, if you have young children. (We have a veritable hamster cemetery in our back yard.) Fish are a good choice if you're willing to keep the tank clean; they're soothing to watch and easy to care for (again, plan cemetery space). Usually, the smaller the animal, the shorter its life.

And think compatibility if you're in the market for more than one pet. A cat plus a gerbil usually equals a crying child. Think about which animals are already at home before you bring in a new addition.

Pet Pests

Flea control is essential. Not only don't you want fleas in your house, but fleas can carry worms into your animal if he inadvertently eats one, and then you have a whole secondary problem to fix. I like monthly applications of Advantage, a chemical you rub in your animal's fur that kills fleas, and there are also carpet cleaning companies who can inject a special salt into your carpet that will kill fleas.

The trick is to keep fleas from breeding, which they do off of your animal (they only hop back on for a quick meal, then it's back into the carpet or your furniture). The right kind of salt injected into your rug will do this. Even if your animal goes outside and brings in more fleas, they'll soon be dead. It's the same with Advantage—you kill the fleas before they have a chance to multiply.

Proper Feeding and Cleaning

What to feed your pet is another decision you'll have to make. It's expensive, but probably the best foods are the chilled ones formulated for maximum nutrition, and available in health food stores and pet clinics. I never go this route. I just use a good, dry kibble, and occasionally mix in a soft variety from the pet food aisle at the grocery store for a treat. I've had dogs and cats live well into their teens on this diet, and I even give them occasional table scraps. Hey, you have no idea what they're eating when they're out of the house, and believe me, you could hardly do worse.

Most animals shed, and the best way to remove animal hair from clothes or furniture is with rubber gloves. Remember to brush animals down outside, vacuum your home frequently, and check all filters. If you don't have any rubber gloves, use loops of masking tape, sticky side out.

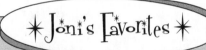

✳ Joni's Favorites ✳

Virtually every other flea-removal plan has been a disaster in my experience. Powders, shampoos, collars, you-name-it, cannot compare to Advantage or professional treatment by FleaBusters (they're the ones who inject the salt into your carpet.).

If your pet throws up or goes potty on your carpet, you'll need to spot clean. There are many carpet sprays that claim to erase animal stains, but check with pet stores for their best recommendations.

Keep pets generally clean and in good health. Bathe dogs every month (cats, as mentioned, will take care of themselves), and keep their sleeping quarters laundered and fresh. When you can't give your dog a water bath, at least rub his coat with baking soda or cornstarch, then brush clean outside. You will avoid "kennel odor" in your house if you take these measures.

Always keep your rabies tag and an ID tag on your pet's collar in case it gets lost. Many people like their vet to install a microchip at the back of their animal's neck, which scanners can read, should their pets get lost or stolen.

Skunk!

If your animal gets sprayed by a skunk, forget that old wives' tale about bathing them in tomato juice. Here's the mixture that really works: In a bucket, combine 1 quart of hydrogen peroxide with ¼ cup baking soda and 1 teaspoon of liquid dish soap. Apply immediately to your pet and rinse with water. But do not try to keep a bottled supply of this, as it produces oxygen and will burst the bottle.

✳ Joni's Favorites ✳

I like a liquid called Nature's Miracle. I dab it in, and wipe it off, then repeat until the stain disappears. Last, vacuum.

Our cat was once sprayed by a skunk, and even after the odor was gone, she stopped grooming herself and her coat began to mat. Rather than put her through the agony of combing out hopelessly knotted fur, I had her anesthetized and let a professional do a quick job of getting her coat smooth again. She was asleep through the whole procedure and woke up beautiful once more and ready to groom herself. (There are also other reasons, such as arthritis or obesity, that can make a cat stop grooming; check with your vet if this problem arises.)

Medicating Pets

What about medicating sick pets? Dogs will take pills more easily than will cats. Simply press the pill into something the dog likes—a pinch of cheese, a slice of meat. Cats, on the other hand, would sooner scratch the living daylights out of you than let you shove something down their throats. Get a friend to help and hold the cat in a thick bag or secure blanket bundle, with only its head exposed. This is to protect you both from getting scratched. Now you have two hands to pry open the mouth and (try) to coax the pill down her throat. You'll probably get bitten anyway, so have a first-aid kit and some hydrogen peroxide handy. My best tip for protecting your hands from sharp teeth and claws (or thorns) is to wear the heavy rubber gardening gloves meant for working with roses.

Chapter Nine

Sparkling Windows and Car Care

✳

nothing says clean like a sparkling mirror or light reflecting through glass. Be sure you read chapters 5 and 6, as they include tips for shining windows and crystal treasures, while chapters 11 and 13 talk specifically about bathrooms and kitchens. But let's discuss windows in greater detail.

Windows

Before you even get to the glass, vacuum the dirt out of any screens with a hand-held vacuum. Now vacuum the windowsills, the back sides of the curtains, and tie back any window treatments so they'll be out of the way.

Is the window basically clean? Remove stickers with warm water and vinegar, and scrape off paint splatters with a pen eraser or a one-sided razor blade (be careful!). If you have aluminum window frames, clean them with silver polish. If your windows or their frames are made of any kind of plastic, do not use ammonia on them; it will dull the finish. If sashes are metal, they can be cleaned with steel wool. It helps to apply a thin coat of oil or Vaseline to the sliding surfaces, to keep them operating smoothly.

If your windows are already stuck shut, hammer a block of wood placed against the sash around the glass. It may loosen dry paint. Don't hammer the sash directly, as this will leave big dents.

The best way to clean windows is with glass cleaner and a squeegee. But also use these tricks of the trade:

> ★ Joni's Favorites ★
>
> Rain-X is a fabulous window cleaner, as rain beads up and leaves the glass relatively clean.

Choose a cool day for cleaning windows. Hot, sunny days make the cleaner dry too quickly, which creates streaks.

Wipe vertically on one side of the window, and horizontally on the other. That way, if you see a streak, you'll know which side it's on.

Some people use air-freshener to clean indoor windows. There's also the added benefit of a fresh scent. Many automotive products translate beautifully to the house. If you put Turtle Wax on shower doors, water will bead up in the future. Likewise, a cup of antifreeze added to your window rinse will prevent formation of frost and ice on windows (although when we lived in the Midwest and experienced temperatures of 70 degrees below zero, I found the crystal formations on the windows exquisite and beautiful).

Notice how much more light floods the room when your windows are clean and the curtains are tied back? Consider whether this elevates your mood (it does mine), and whether you might want a simpler window treatment that allows more sunshine to fill the room. Or if you have an area where too much light is overheating your home or causing carpet and furniture to sun-bleach, consider coating your window with reflective film, installing seasonal screens to block out some light, or putting up a heavier curtain.

Heavy Metal

Keep all silver, copper, brass, and chrome shining. Chrome you can clean with a swipe of rubbing alcohol; for polishing finer metals, see chapter 6.

Listen to Your Mother!

In your trunk, keep a car repair kit with a flashlight, flares, empty one-gallon gasoline container, and jumper cables. If you live where your car could get stuck in snow or mud, either keep a bag of cat litter or a square of carpet for providing traction under the tires (floor mats also work). To prepare for being stranded anywhere, include a small emergency package containing a solar blanket, a wool blanket, a transistor radio with fresh batteries, an extra jacket, tennis shoes, and fairly nonperishable food, such as granola bars. (You do not want the papers to run a story about "The Local Resident Who Stayed Alive Eating Car Upholstery.")

Another good item to include in your trunk is a towel for wiping down your car after a car wash, or if a light rain could water-spot it.

To keep groceries from rolling around in the trunk, put your bags in a plastic bin in your trunk. Especially if you live alone, you'll rarely buy enough groceries to pack a trunk, and this keeps items from breaking and spilling.

What else needs to shine? Look at hardware—hinges, knobs, faucets, latches, and so on—and make sure you wipe them with the appropriate cleaner. Check lamps, fireplace screens, television screens, and any objects that could reflect light, such as a porcelain bowl or a glazed flower pot. When you've shined the shiny things, everything else looks cleaner and you're ready for company.

Keeping Your Car Clean

Keep car registration, maps, and so on in your glove box and don't let them get strewn about the car. A great item to include there is a package of wet wipes; they always come in handy.

See if you can buy a miniature version of your city phone book and yellow pages; this makes it easy to look up numbers, addresses, and where that great restaurant was. Tuck it under the passenger seat.

Keep trash contained so you don't have leaves, wrappers, receipts, and Tic-Tacs all over the place.

Wash your car (or have it washed) regularly and vacuum it out. Before you begin, check out the exterior. Remove any rust with S.O.S pads or kerosene. Linseed oil will take off tar. A vinegar-and-water solution will get winter salt out of floor mats.

Tip: Remove bumper stickers from your car with nail polish remover.

If washing the car yourself, fill a bucket with sudsy water (I use dishwashing liquid, as detergents are too harsh for paint), and work quickly—don't choose a hot day or the soap will dry too fast. A stiff brush should help clean headlights, grills, hubcaps, and bumpers. A sponge should take care of the body. I rinse with a hose, starting at the top and working my way down. Now, still working fairly quickly, dry your car from top to bottom. Towels are fine, but a leather chamois is great to wring out and reuse as you go. Last, clean windows and mirrors with regular glass cleaner.

Tip

Keep your car battery clean by pouring soda water (or soda pop) over the battery. Protect for the future with an application of Vaseline.

Periodically wipe down the interior of your car—the dashboard, armrests, and so on with Armor-All. It cleans and shines. Use saddle soap to clean leather seats. Then, if you like a fragrant car, keep a scented sachet under the seat.

Chapter Ten

This Box Called Home

Ever notice how empty houses seem to know it, and fall apart on their own? Stairs get rickety, ceilings fall in, and linoleum curls. It's as if the house is dying of loneliness. Yet, if people live in the house, it seems to hold together and almost enjoy the presence of humans. The same goes for apartments.

This chapter is about preserving the structure you inhabit, making sure the physical container you live in lasts. There are many repairs you can make yourself, and easy ways to insure that you'll live in a pleasant atmosphere. Even if you're renting, it's good to know how to make repairs, in case you can't rely on the owner to do so.

Temperature

Maintain a comfortable temperature. If you're living alone, this should be easy, but the minute two people share a living space, it can become a point of contention. Try to make a compromise you can live with.

Part of comfort is the humidity level. If you live in an unusually dry climate, you may want to invest in a humidifier, and if you live in a wet climate, place tubs of absorbing, dehumidifying crystals in damp basements and other moist spots. If your basement is especially damp, make sure your gutters are not clogged, which allows water to seep into the foundation.

While humidifiers can help tremendously (and save furniture from cracking, too), they can be real troublemakers if they're not kept scrupulously clean. Molds and bacteria can thrive in the tray and water tank, so clean yours at least weekly. Use a mixture of diluted bleach (1 teaspoon of chlorine bleach to 1 gallon of water), and let it soak twenty minutes. Mineral deposits can be removed with vinegar, and a small brush can loosen any buildup.

Tip

Lower your energy bill by turning down your hot-water heater to 120 degrees instead of 140 degrees.

Twice a year, check your heating and air-conditioning units. Replace filters monthly if yours tend to fill with dust or hair.

To save money on heating and cooling, make sure windows are tightly sealed. Recaulk them if necessary. To determine whether a draft is entering, light a match and see if it flickers when you hold it near the seal.

If you have oil burners or heat pumps that stop working, try pressing the reset button on the front of the machine; it may be all that's needed.

Fireplaces are deceiving; when lit, they actually suck warm air from your home and send it out the chimney. So be careful and watch that your hard-earned money doesn't go up in smoke. When you're ready to clean a fireplace, open the damper to draw out dust, and shovel the ashes into a paper bag. Vacuum out the rest. Now scrub brickwork with a stiff brush, and clean any glass on the fireplace screen with glass cleaner. Close the damper. (If your fireplace is not in use, it's a great place to display an assortment of candles or a pretty plant.)

Never turn on gas and then go looking for a match. I must confess I did this once. Relatives were coming for Christmas, and I wanted a roaring fire in the fireplace to look cozy and inviting when they arrived. There was just one hitch: my husband had always lit our gas fireplace and he wasn't home yet. (Another reason to know how to do everything yourself.)

No problem, I figured. I'll just crank on the gas like he does, then light it with one of those trigger lighter things. Now, where did he put the lighter? Well, I found it, but not quickly enough. As soon as I flicked the lighter, I heard the whoosh of billowing brightness, engulfing me in flame. I remembered to stop, drop, and roll, but did I mention that I was nine months pregnant? I looked like a beached whale.

Fortunately, the house didn't catch fire—but I did. I burned off my bangs, eyebrows, eyelashes, and nose hairs. My nose was bright red (à la Rudolph), and my hair was coming off in clumps of what appeared to be tar. There wasn't anything Christmasy or inviting about the situation when my relatives arrived. So learn from my mistakes, and save roasting for turkeys.

Hinges and Slides

Check all doors and drawers to make sure they operate smoothly and quietly. WD-40, or even cooking spray, will lubricate squeaky hinges. As mentioned earlier, soap or wax will lubricate sticking drawers. Graphite from a pencil might help also. If you try this and you still have a stuck door, you might

Listen to Your Mother!

If natural gas heats your water and stove, you'll want to make sure the pilot lights stay lit at all times. Should yours go out, here's what to do:

Combination Gas Control System (newer furnaces)

* Set room thermostat to lowest setting.

* Unplug electricity to your furnace.

* Clean out any dust or lint in furnace chamber.

* Check gas control knob. It should say OFF. If not, turn it to OFF and allow chamber to air out for five minutes.

* Hold a long, lit fireplace match next to the pilot burner (you may have to open a door to do this). Don't put your hand in, and don't turn on the gas before the match is in place.

* Turn the gas control knob to PILOT. Push it down and hold it; the pilot should ignite.

* Close all panels.

* Plug electricity back in.

* Set room thermostat to highest setting. Most furnaces will respond within 45 seconds.

* Once the furnace is on, set heat to desired setting.

Manifold Gas Control System (older furnaces)

* Set room thermostat to lowest setting.

need to take it off its hinges and remove rust from the hinge pin. Here's how to take a door off its hinges (this is easy). With a hammer and screwdriver, tap upward under the head of the pin. It will slide up out of the hinges, and you can pull the door out of position and set it to one side. Remove the rust with steel

+ Unplug electricity to your furnace.

+ Clean out any dust or lint in furnace chamber.

+ Make sure main gas valve is off. If you have a pilot valve, make sure it's off, also. Allow chamber to air out for five minutes.

+ Hold a long, lit fireplace match next to the pilot burner (you may have to open a door to do this). Don't put your hand in, and don't turn on the gas before the match is in place.

+ If you don't have a pilot valve, turn the main gas valve and the pilot should ignite. Let it burn for two minutes.

+ If you do have a pilot valve, turn it on. The pilot should ignite. Let it burn for two minutes. (You may have to hold down a plunger button or turn a reset device after lighting the pilot, to get gas to flow to the burners.) Then turn the main gas valve to the ON position.

+ Close all panels.

+ Plug electricity back in.

+ Set room thermostat to highest setting. Most furnaces will respond within 45 seconds.

+ Once the furnace is on, set heat to desired setting.

If you smell gas, do not stay in your home; go outside to call the gas company.

wool, then lightly oil the pin. Realign the hinge plates and tap the pin down through them with your hammer.

In general, check all screws and fasteners to make sure they aren't loose.

Tip

When turning handles or tightening screws, remember Left is Loose and Right is Tight.

Tighten towel racks, banisters, knobs, and electrical plates. Install new washers in leaky faucets.

Ceilings and Walls

Take note of ceiling and wall conditions—are there any cracks? Some could be the result of a house settling, but some might indicate a leaky roof, termites, or dry rot in your foundation. Have suspicious areas checked by a professional.

✳ Joni's Favorites ✳

To patch chips in plaster and sheet-rock walls, smooth over with Dap, Fixall, or Erase-a-Hole for smaller holes. If your walls are white, you might get away with not even painting over the patch.

Clean walls with mild soap and water, or an all-purpose cleaning spray for enamel paint. Always check to make sure your cleaner won't remove paint. Semigloss enamel is the easiest to keep clean; its shiny surface wipes off easily and it's often the choice for kitchen and bathroom walls, all doors, and woodwork. You could even consider high gloss for doors and woodwork. But most people opt for a flat finish on all other walls, especially ceilings, because a matte finish hides blemishes and imperfections much better than shiny paint (just like powdering your nose).

Painting

Paint is one of the cheapest and fastest ways to freshen or change the look of a room—and mistakes are not terribly costly. You can always select a new paint for just a few dollars. But don't scrimp; get a more expensive brand that will cover in one coat—you'll need less and you'll save half the time in labor.

When choosing a color other than neutrals, select a softer shade than the sofa fabric you might be matching. A small paint chip of coral may be more intense than you think and turn into a wall of hot pink. A touch of gray mixed into the color usually softens it and will make your fabric stand out, instead of it looking washed out against a bright wall.

Tip — Remove paint from hair with baby oil.

To get ready to paint, tape off all woodwork and windows, and put down drop cloths. Unscrew switch plates. Remove all dirt, cobwebs, and so on, and fill nail holes. Sand down plaster patches or rough spots. Sometimes it takes longer to prep than to actually paint, but it's worth it. Vaseline rubbed on doorknobs will keep paint from splattering them, and wet newspaper will adhere to windows to keep paint off the glass.

If you can't finish the job in one session, wrap your brushes and roller securely in plastic to prevent them from drying out. To get rid of lingering paint odor, place a dish of vinegar in the room.

Tip — Soak stained fingernails in denture cleaner to whiten them.

Consider texturing your walls by dabbing the paint on with a sponge, or following a wet paint application with a dab of a scrunched-up plastic bag. Strokes of a plastic comb can create a great texture, too. Mixing sand into the paint will give it a nubby effect. Experiment on sheets of newspaper before you begin on the actual wall.

If you've used latex paint, clean-up will be easy with soap and water. Oil-based paint will wash off your hands with baby or salad oil.

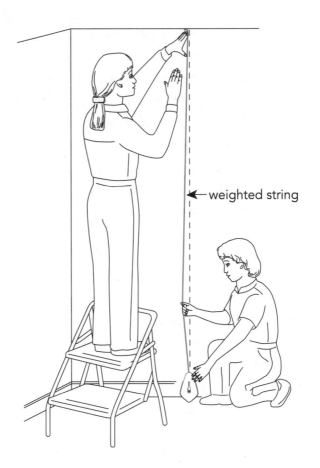

← weighted string

Wallpapering

Wallpaper is a fast way to brighten up a room and give it some pizzazz. It also hides flaws that paint cannot. I've hung dozens of rolls of wallpaper, and here's how to make it easy.

First of all, just as with painting, prepare your walls. Remove any previous wallpaper with vinegar and hot water, or with fabric softener diluted in hot water. If you'll be using a pattern with a dark background, paint your walls that color first, so seams won't show. When the walls are dry, apply wallpaper sizing—or a thinned-out mixture of wallpaper paste and water. Just slosh it on; it doesn't have to be perfect because you'll be covering it up.

If you've selected a pattern with a large repeating design, you'll use more paper in order to match the seams, so order an extra double-bolt.

When the sizing is dry, you're ready to apply the paper. First you need to mark a straight, vertical line, and the best way is with a plumb line. You can buy one at a hardware store or make your own. To do it yourself, coat a string with a piece of colored chalk, and simply hang a weight from one end. To mark the plumb line, hold the string up high against the wall. Let it stop swinging, and have someone hold the weight against the wall near the bottom, too. Now pluck the string and the chalk will mark a true vertical line on the wall. Line the edge of your wallpaper up against this line, not against a corner of the wall itself, as your house is probably not perfectly square.

Begin in an inconspicuous corner, if you can, as the pattern may not match perfectly when you work your way around the room and arrive at your beginning spot. To make it less obvious, use scissors to cut around flowers or patterns, and overlap them to conceal distinct edge lines.

The reason everybody's afraid of wallpapering is because they've seen old comedies about wallpaper strips falling on the workmen's heads and wrapping around them in a gluey mess. This need never happen to you and here's how: paint the paste onto the wall, not onto the paper. Use a roller brush if you like. Paint it about the width of one strip of paper at a time. Now, as you put each strip in place, you are handling dry paper, and you can scoot it around on the wall until you get it where you want it. Believe me, the wall does not think and does not know

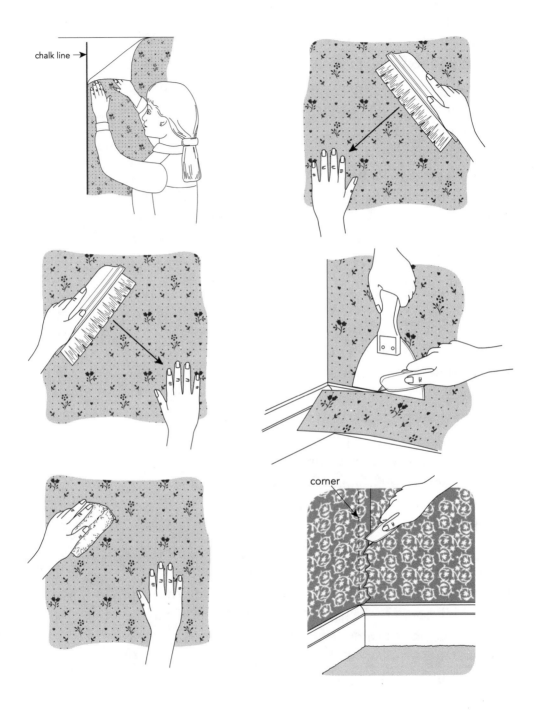

whether the paste was placed directly on the wall or got there from the wallpaper.

Many wallpapers boast that they are prepasted and just need to be dunked into water. I've found they simply don't stick as well, and you have to work very quickly so they won't dry out. Instead, I ignore the label and put paste on them anyway, and so do professional paper hangers.

Now, using a wide, stiff wallpaper brush, begin at the center of the strip of paper and smooth it out to each side, using X strokes. You'll know if you're using too much paste; it will squish out the seams. If you're using too little, the seams will be dry and you'll need to apply additional paste under the edges.

Next, use a straight edge and a razor knife to cut the top and bottom off at the ceiling and baseboard edges. Use a seam roller to make seams tight. If you have air bubbles, try to smooth them out before they dry. Sometimes you can slit them with a razor blade and press them flat. Last, wipe off the entire strip with a clean, wet sponge.

Tip Believe it or not: You can clean soiled wallpaper by rubbing it with slices of bread.

Before you replace switch plates and plug covers, wrap them with the same wallpaper, matching the pattern up, so they'll virtually disappear when replaced.

If you want an inexpensive border, buy a roll of vertically striped paper, then cut it into strips and hang it at the top of your walls. This also draws attention upward and makes your ceilings seem higher. Most border rolls cover just fifteen feet, whereas you can multiply that many times over by cutting up a roll of regular wallpaper.

Other Wall Treatments

To jazz up plain walls, stenciling on a border is another option, and it's not hard to do. Look at the stencils in craft aisles; they can add a lot of personality to a room with minimal expense. The paint you use comes in jars and has the consistency of lipstick—you daub it on with a blunt brush made especially for stenciling. My best tip here: if you're working with a stencil that has fruit, leaves, petals, or any items that need shading, use two or three colors within one stencil hole to give it a more realistic and artistic look.

Nail holes in a white wall can be disguised with white toothpaste.

Upholstering is another wall treatment to consider, especially if you want to muffle sound or if you have gravely imperfect walls. Now, don't panic; I know this sounds expensive and difficult to do, but it doesn't have to be. It's also a great fire-retardant if you use the proper batting under your fabric.

Here's all you do. Buy enough one-inch thick, flame-retardant batting to cover your walls, and staple it on, top and bottom, with a staple gun. This is incredibly easy. Next, choose a fabric you can afford. Shop the remnants and sales; it doesn't have to be imported silk. Cut it into the lengths of your wall, and sew the side seams together, matching prints if necessary. Now staple it onto the walls, covering the "stuffing." Make your own welting (the cheapest way to go) or purchase a welting or braiding that goes with your fabric, and hot glue it onto the tops and bottoms of your walls, to conceal the staples and the raw edges of the fabric. That is it.

An even less expensive way to upholster is to do just the top half of the wall, say in a dining room. Just attach the fabric, put a strip of molding for a chair rail under it, then paint the wall below.

If you choose a beautiful print for your wall, you may not need to hang any paintings on it to complete the look you want. But if your fabric is plain or textured, you might want to hang a picture without puncturing a hole in the fabric. The way to do this is to hang the picture from a thick ribbon, then nail the ribbon to the very top of the wall. Add a bow to finish off the ribbon's top edge.

Lighting

Examine the lighting in your rooms—is it bright enough where you need to work, such as in the kitchen? Can it be softened in the bedroom? Install dimmer switches if you want to soften bright lighting or create mood in a dining room.

Track or spot lighting is attractive on paintings and other objects you wish to highlight. Indirect lighting is most pleasant where you simply want to create overall lighting.

If you need to add lighting, shop carefully. You don't want to add so many lamps that you overcrowd plugs or dominate the room with huge lamps when a wall sconce would do. Sketch out the floor plan of your room and ask for help at a lighting store. Don't get talked into a beautiful lighting system that has ten-dollar bulbs you'll need to replace frequently. And consider the color of the light bulbs—you can get a fluorescent look, a pink cast, a daylight effect, and a dozen other light "colors."

Tip Fill stripped screw holes with toothpicks and wood glue; let dry.

If you're replacing a lamp shade, use this rule of thumb: divide the height of the lamp base by three, and that's how tall the shade should be. Its width should be double the width of the lamp base. This formula will keep you from buying a lamp shade that looks out of proportion. Do not use worn or frayed cords, and do not overload your wall plugs.

If your lights won't come on, the first thing to check is if the bulb is burned out or loose. Next, check the fuse box, which has switches that control the power going into the house. If one of the switches is clicked "off," try turning it back on. (Always switch off, then on.) This may solve the problem. If not, a fuse may need replacing. You can either call an electrician or learn to do this yourself.

To remove a broken light bulb, turn off the electricity, then twist a potato or a rubber ball into the fixture, then remove it with the broken bottom.

Another possibility is that your lights may be controlled by another light switch in the house, which is in the off position. Or, if you have a newer home, it could have ground fault circuit interrupters (GFCIs) to protect against shock from bathroom appliances, such as blow dryers, and you'll need to see if the power is out in more than one bathroom.

If there's a real blackout and the electricity is off, know where flashlights, candles, and matches are. Don't open your refrigerator and let any cold out. Make sure you own a clock radio that switches over to batteries if the electricity quits (and make sure it has batteries).

Plumbing

What if a pipe should leak, freeze, or burst? I just had a pipe burst under a bathroom, and it can cause major problems.

Turn your water off immediately at the main shut-off. If you're renting, call your landlord. If you own your house and don't know where the main shut-off valve is, check with your real estate agent, who can probably tell you. In any case, you should know how to turn off all water and gas supplies in the event of an emergency.

If a pipe has only a small leak, dry it and tie a rubber glove around the leak, then cover it thoroughly with duct tape. This is only a temporary solution, but it may hold it until you can get it fixed by a plumber. If the pipe has frozen or burst, turn off the main water supply and call a plumber immediately. If the burst is not causing immediate damage, take a few minutes to fill your bathtub, as you may need this for a water source over the next few days. Don't flush any toilets unless you absolutely must. Your tub of water now becomes your emergency water source for drinking, cooking, and flushing if necessary.

For stopped up sinks and other bathroom-related problems, see chapter 11.

Appliances

What if you have a major appliance that isn't working right? If you rent, call your landlord to see if he or she will handle the repair or reimburse you for doing so. Either way, before calling in a repairperson, call the manufacturer's 800 number. Many of the major name brands offer step-by-step repair instructions over the phone.

If a dishwasher seems to have power but isn't doing a good job, try running the kitchen sink water until it's hot before you turn on the dishwasher. This flushes the cold water out of the system and your dishes will be cleaner. What if leaks are a problem? The most common cause of leaks is too much dish-washing detergent.

If your clothes washer is filling too slowly with water, you may need to replace the hose screens. To do this, turn off the

Listen to Your Mother!

Whether you rent or own, but especially if you own, you will want to develop a reliable list of handypersons, plumbers, electricians, and such. Begin by asking neighbors and friends for referrals of good, trustworthy workers so you can avoid wildly thumbing through the yellow pages in an emergency. A good handyman can do everything from helping you assemble a bed frame to fixing the spring on your screen door. Then there are certain projects that simply require a professional because of the scale of the work involved or the complexity.

There are two kinds of contractors—licensed and unlicensed—and they are priced accordingly. If you choose to hire an unlicensed contractor, you'll save money. But if you're

not happy with the work, you will have no legal recourse. A licensed contractor, though more expensive, has to meet legal codes and standards or risk losing his or her license.

My husband is a closet architect and an admitted remodel-a-holic (his only flaw), and we are constantly remodeling some part of our house. This means I have seen approximately three million tool-belted workers bent over, exposing more of their backsides than I have ever wished to see. Nevertheless, despite living with constant disruption and disarray, I always love the final result of Bob's ideas.

It also means that we've hired more than our share of both licensed and unlicensed contractors, and we've found that success basically comes down to the worker machine and the water supply, unscrew the hoses, and replace the screens with new ones from the hardware store. Now screw the hoses back in, turn on the water, and you're set to go. What if your clothes simply aren't coming clean? You may be packing the washer too full, or you might need a water softener.

him- or herself. So keep these things in mind before you hire:

1. Meet the contractor. Does the person seem reliable, and if you are hiring the contractor for a big project, can you live with this person in your house every day?

2. Check out the contractor's work. Don't just look at photos in a book; go personally and see other jobs he or she has done. Talk with other customers.

3. Find out who he or she hires as helpers. Will the contractor be on site during the work?

4. Request a bid on the total job, rather than having the contractor charge by the hour.

5. If the contractor is to provide his or her own materials, get that in writing.

6. Sketch out the plan on paper to reduce the chance of a misunderstanding.

7. Make sure workers clean up after themselves. You don't want painters leaving drop cloths, cans, and ladders for you to trip over.

8. If a fair amount of rubbish will be generated, such as happens when you tear down a wall, who will be responsible for its disposal?

9. Will your contractor guarantee results—and come back if there's some adjusting needed after he or she is through? (There almost always is.)

10. Don't pay in full until the job is done.

Likewise, if they're taking too long to dry, the dryer might simply be on the wrong setting—always troubleshoot before you call in an expensive repairperson.

If an older oven stops working, reset its clock. Sometimes that's the only problem. If the oven smokes when you use it, it's probably time for a cleaning; food spills could be burned on the racks and bottom. If the oven door won't open after you've run it through the self-cleaning cycle, you just need to wait for it to cool down again.

Storage

Now look for unused storage space—could bins fit under your bed or nightstand? Could a shelf be installed above the rod in your closet? If you have stairs, there may be space there for a bookcase, or even a mini-office. If you're open to the idea of a little dust and plaster, hire a contractor to make use of stud space by a telephone, a desk, a medicine cabinet, at your bedside—wherever you could use a couple of 16-inch-wide shelves. They're not terribly deep, but deep enough to hold phone books, folded towels, bedside reading, some cookware, a safe, or pretty storage boxes.

Tip: The best way to find more space is to remember the letters in the word "space." S = Sort, P = Purge, A = Assign a spot, C = Containers, and E = Enjoy!

Another place to "find" storage is above your doorways. A shelf installed near the ceiling is great for storing items you need, but don't need handy—such as an extra quilt for company, books you're not ready to part with, seasonal items held in a decorative box.

Shallow containers are great to push under the bed, and hold seasonal clothes, shoes, sports equipment, scrapbooks, legal records, and other items you want, but may not want on your desktop.

Remember to utilize space under end tables—use a round table covered with a floor-length cloth, and you'll have several cubic feet of storage for a drum-sized container or two.

A way to increase space in children's rooms is to use bunkbeds. If only one child has the room, use just the top bunk, and put a desk or play space beneath it. Run a high shelf all the way around the room, a foot below the ceiling. This is a great place to store toys and other items out of the way.

Storage can also be found inside closet doors—these are good places for shoebags, hooks, and hanging containers that can hold purses, umbrellas, hats, and scarves.

Look around your home and analyze every wall and corner. Is there wasted space that could hide your CDs, your electric mixer, your shaving gear? Sometimes a standing screen can almost create a new room or workspace, by blocking it off from the rest of the room. I know of a woman who took the mattress out of her sofa-sleeper and used that space for storing holiday decorations!

Tip

Always keep records of any remodeling you do, and take before-and-after photos. Someday you might sell your house and scale down—and if so, you'll be hit with capital gains taxes. However, if you've documented the improvements you've made, you can deduct the expenses you incurred making your house worth more.

If you never use your fireplace, store something inside it and hide it with a pretty screen, fan, or plant.

Could ready-made cupboards be mounted on a blank kitchen wall? These are easy to install, and cost much less than custom-made cabinets.

Is there room at the end of your bed for a trunk or chest? There's a world of storage space in these, and they can be topped with a pretty cushion for additional seating in the bedroom.

Part Three

The Rooms

Chapter Eleven

Bathroom

Like most people, this is the room I least like to clean. But there are ways to make the job easier and something you will look forward to. Well, maybe I exaggerate that last point.

Clean as You Go

First of all, the easiest way to maintain a clean bath is to clean as you go. As I mentioned earlier, every time you use the bathroom, leave no trace that you were there. Take a few seconds to wipe splashes off the faucet and counters, straighten towels, and so on. Corral belongings into decorative bowls, boxes, or baskets so the counters aren't cluttered. Put away toothpaste, combs, and toiletries. Don't leave damp towels on the counter where they'll stay wet and grow bacteria; hang them up so air can circulate. This way, you won't have a germy, uninviting bathroom, and when it's time for a thorough cleaning, the job will be much easier.

Plumbing Repairs

Next, make sure everything's working (or you'll mess up a newly cleaned bathroom if a plumber needs to be called). Are any sink drains stopped up? You can buy liquids that unclog drains, or try dropping in three Alka-Seltzer tablets, then a cup of vinegar. Wait a few minutes, then flush with hot water. If this doesn't work, sometimes you can use a plunger to clear the sink, or run a "snake" down the drain, which you can purchase at a hardware store.

If faucets are leaky, replace the washer. If a leak persists, talk it over with experts at the hardware store, and last of all, call a plumber. If the water coming from your faucet doesn't seem to be flowing strongly enough, you may need to clean the aerator,

Listen to Your Mother!

I am going to settle a dispute once and for all. The toilet paper should unroll from the top, not from the bottom. If you buy a patterned or embossed toilet paper, you will see that the pattern rolls out upside-down if you have the roll turned the wrong way. Furthermore, you can make a dressier guest bath if you fold the paper into a point that rests on the roll, making it that much easier to get hold of. This is impossible if the end is hiding behind the roll.

My husband once began a speech about marriage by holding up a toilet paper roll, and saying, "Which way does it go, guys?" Everyone burst out laughing because they've all had the same household argument. You now, however, have the definitive answer.

and you can do this yourself without calling in a pro. First, wrap the aerator (the thing the water comes out of) with masking tape to protect its finish from scratches if you need to use a wrench. Now turn it clockwise and take it off. Don't worry; this whole thing will reassemble in a snap. Now check the washer. If it's worn, replace it. Then clean the aerator by holding it upside down beneath running water. If minerals have built up, remove them with a toothbrush or a pin. Now reinstall the aerator by screwing it back on counterclockwise. Peel off the tape. Ta-da!

What if the toilet keeps running? This is a super easy fix. Remove the lid from the toilet tank. Possibly the rubber ball (flapper) isn't connecting as it should at the base of the tank. Maybe it's worn and needs replacing. Or maybe you just need to reconnect the chain that holds the mechanism in place.

Is the toilet plugged? If so, you'll need to plunge it. First, gather a stack of five or six paper towels and just keep them handy. Shove the plunger at the hole several times, creating a vacuum and continuing to plunge. In a minute you should hear the workings of the toilet starting up again. Lift the plunger and see if the water swirls down and away. Flush to make sure it's really working. Now, wait—you're not through yet—you're holding a germy, yucky tool and you need to store it properly. First, flush an extra time just to clean the plunger off—let the water swirl inside and shake it out well in the toilet. Now, hold a bucket or your stack of paper towels beneath the plunger so it won't drip on the floor. Quickly replace it in the receptacle where you keep it, throw away the paper towels, and wash your hands with a good disinfecting soap. I always spray my plunger with Lysol as I put it away, too.

Before I clean the bathroom, I toss about three denture tablets (or Alka-Seltzer) into the toilet to fizz and clean while I'm doing everything else, then I clean the toilet last.

How is the shower head running—too slow? This could be low water pressure in the first place, due to mineral build-up in old pipes (and it's why copper pipes are best, if you're ever building a new house). Or maybe the shower head is clogged. Unscrew it and soak it overnight in vinegar to remove minerals.

If your shower isn't draining very fast, you need to degunk the strainer. I know, it's disgusting, but no one's going to do it for you. Unscrew the strainer and lift it off. Clean it thoroughly. Clean as far as you can reach into the pipe, removing hair and so on. Now put the strainer back, and screw the ring back on.

Tubs and Showers

Now it's time to actually clean the bathroom. Let's tackle the tub and shower first. If yours is fiberglass, just wipe it clean with shampoo and water. Put a little car wax on fiberglass walls, and you'll prevent soap buildup. If your tub is porcelain, use a nonabrasive cleaner, such as Bon Ami or SoftScrub. For stubborn rings, you can make a paste of hydrogen peroxide and cream of tartar, smear it on and let it dry, then rinse it off. If you have a sliding shower door, tracks can be cleaned with vinegar (let them soak for a couple of hours, then scrub). Keep tracks running smoothly with a dab of floor polish.

For tile surfaces, use vinegar, or cleaners that remove soap scum, lime, or mildew. For reaching high shower walls, use a sponge mop. I never use bleach on grout; it will eventually turn it yellow. But if you do need to work on grout, scrub it with an old toothbrush and the appropriate cleaner. Shower sprays are great for keeping up daily. And I always squeegee my tiles to get the moisture off them and insure spot-free drying.

I prefer a shower curtain to a sliding door. First of all, there are no tracks to collect minerals and pose cleaning problems. Second, you can toss a plastic curtain into the washing machine with a couple of towels, then hang it to dry, which is much easier than trying to degunk doors. And third, it's more decorative. If your plastic curtain has any mineral build-up on it, just add a cup of vinegar to the wash cycle. The way to use a shower curtain is to have two—a plastic one that hangs inside the tub when you're showering so water will run off and into the tub, and a fabric one that hangs outside the tub, to be pretty and provide additional privacy. Make sure they're dry, then tie them both back. This also will make your bathroom look larger, as the line of sight won't be blocked by a closed shower door.

Tip

Some experts say that to whiten grout, use a paste of baking soda, water, and a few drops of bleach.

Counters and Sinks

Is there a window in your bathroom that needs cleaning? A curtain you can clean with a hand-held vacuum? Do that next.

Now let's wipe down the windowsills, counters, and sinks. Be sure your cleaner disinfects as you go. If minerals have built up at the base of your faucets, use the same trick as for shower door tracks—a good soaking of vinegar. To clean chrome faucets, use clean coffee filters, baby wipes, rubbing alcohol, or used laundry softening sheets. Hair spray will come off mirrors with a spritz of rubbing alcohol.

Mirrors

Use glass cleaner to shine mirrors (don't forget your hand mirror) and medicine cabinet mirror. This is a good time to see what needs tossing from the medicine cabinet and drawers. Throw away old makeup and any lotions or oils that have become rancid. Flush expired medicine down the toilet.

Toilets

Last, spray toilet cleaner into the toilet bowl, scrub inside both rim and bowl, then swish and flush. If you have a stubborn toilet ring, use a pumice stone on it. (Prevent such rings by placing a capful of chlorine bleach in the toilet tank every week.) Now spray the exterior and lid of the toilet with antibacterial spray and wipe it down. Close the toilet lid. Is there a man in your house? If so, check any wall surfaces near the toilet to make sure they're wiped clean and disinfected, too.

Joni's Favorites

A good commercial product for mildew is Tilex.

The age-old discussion about men leaving the toilet seat up has always mystified me—where were these people raised? Everybody, men and women both, should close the lid when the toilet's not in use. They can then raise what they need to when they go in to use it. Not only will this contain bacteria better, but aesthetically it looks much nicer to enter a bathroom where the toilet lid is closed rather than one exposing this unattractive hole of water.

To eliminate bathroom odors, simply light a match or a scented candle.

Final Touches

When you've finished cleaning, go ahead and dry your hands on the bathroom towels; you're going to gather them all up and launder them when you're through, anyway. Pick up any bathmats or towels used for the floor and launder those as well.

Empty the trash, rinse out the wastebasket, and spray it with disinfectant.

Clean the bathroom floor, using the appropriate cleaner for whatever surface you have (see chapter 7). Be very careful if your floor is slippery when wet, and dry it with a rag to prevent slips. If you're thinking of replacing your bathroom floor, be sure to use rough-surfaced material, such as non-shiny tile or slabs of rock; they'll be less dangerous. I don't recommend wood because of potential wood damage in such a watery environment.

Finally, replace old towels with clean ones, and check your supplies of soap and facial and toilet tissues. Do any light bulbs need replacing? You're done! Unless you've had mineral deposits to work on, or a major plumbing mishap, you can probably completely clean most bathrooms in just fifteen minutes.

How to Create a Welcoming Guest Bath

Did you know that many Victorian and Greek Revival homes were built with no toilet facilities on the main floor? I know this is true because I lived in one. The idea was that you visited someone briefly for tea, but you never had the audacity to stay so long that you had to ask to use the facilities. One did not discuss bodily functions, my dear. (In our home, a coat closet had finally been converted into a half-bath on the main floor.)

Today, it's a sign of hospitality to provide guests with a comfortable powder room in which to freshen up. If at all possible, try not to make this the "family bathroom" as well.

✳ Joni's Favorites ✳

I love Rain-X for cleaning shower doors; it makes the water just bead up and wipe off. (Baby oil will do the same trick.)

A clean toilet, sink, and counter, polished faucets, and an empty wastebasket are just the beginning (and if your guest is not staying overnight, they won't need much else). Spruce up a bit in here—add a blooming plant, try a daring wallpaper, or place a pretty art object on the counter. Don't go too far. Towels look cute tied with a bow, but they're not terribly practical.

To make overnight guests feel genuinely welcome, you might also provide anything they may have forgotten, such as shampoo, a toothbrush, or a small bottle of lotion. These can be available—new in their wrappers—in a small basket. Have plenty of extra tissue, tampons, and washcloths in a cupboard, and a drinking glass near the sink. Pretty soaps, a vase of flowers, a night light, and a fluffy towel are all appreciated. If there's room on the counter (remember, overnight guests also need a place for their own toiletry bag), add a bowl of fruit or a plate of sweets, and perhaps something cool to drink, on ice.

Hang an extra terry cloth robe on a hook on the back of the door, and leave out a new pair of slippers. If you have a tub, place bath salts, a scented candle, and some magazines in a rack nearby. A breakfast tray waiting on a turned-down bed can hold a rose, a newspaper, a television guide, a bedtime snack, even a "menu" of tomorrow's breakfast, and a weather report. Any of these extra touches are sure to make your guests feel pampered!

Chapter Twelve

Bedroom

✳

a third of your life will be spent in the bedroom, and even though you'll be fast asleep, that's precisely why you need to make it as relaxing as you can: so you can in fact get a good night's rest.

A Room Just for Sleeping

When you were a kid, your bedroom was the only place that was all yours—you may have had your desk in there for doing homework, your toys for playing, and all kinds of exciting stuff on the walls. Everything you owned was crammed into that room. But now you have an entire house or apartment for those things, and you can designate one room *just for sleeping*.

Lighting

The lighting in your bedroom is an important part of the atmosphere. While you may want bright light for when you're cleaning, you also need the option of soft lighting that sets the stage for sleep. Dimmer wall switches, or lamps with bright-ness controls, are ideal.

If outside sunlight wakes you too early, install black-out cur-tains or shades. By the way, a great tip for keeping pin-holes of light from coming through curtains is to paint the holes on the back with a correction fluid, such as Liquid Paper or White Out.

A Feast for the Senses

Many of us respond to fragrance, and you may want to dab lightbulbs with scented oil, keep a vase of fresh flowers on the nightstand, or keep a bowl of potpourri in the room. Just make sure it's a soothing scent, not one that makes you want to dash into the kitchen for a slice of apple pie! Some people find the smell of lavender sleep-inducing. Others are allergic to fragrances and need the absence of any scent.

Listen to Your Mother!

Think of the atmosphere in your room as a visual massage: What colors, shapes, and patterns are most soothing to your eye? Bright splashes of red and purple may look jazzy in a department store window, but will you really feel sleepy in a Mardi Gras-themed bed-room? Look at paint samples and see which ones make you feel invig-orated. Now, throw those away. Most people select soft, restful shades for the bedroom—blues, greens, and pastels usually have a calming effect. It doesn't matter whether you choose paint, wallpa-per, or even bright colors, as long as your physical reaction to them is one of relaxation: You want to walk in and think, "Ahh . . ."

Billowing fabric often creates a lushness and cushiony feel to a room. You can create this effect with long drapes that puddle on the floor, tablecloths on your nightstands, lengths of fabric wrapped around bedposts or curtain rods, or a comfortable throw tossed over a soft chair.

Sound is so important to our sleep—our hearing is the first part of us to wake up, and sudden noises can ruin a wonderful cycle of rest. (All the more reason for decorating with lots of fabrics, which absorb sound.) If you're disturbed by noise, consider getting one of those machines that emit "white noise," a static-like constant hum that muffles sudden sounds. These machines usually have additional settings for rain, birds, creeks, and other soothing sounds. Even the steady hum of static on the radio, or an electric fan, can provide the muffling necessary to let you sleep. If music relaxes you, you might also consider putting an unobtrusive stereo system in your room.

Tip Warm feet help you sleep better. Instead of lying there, shivering, and waiting for your feet to warm up, soak them briefly in hot water. Water's a great conductor of heat, and your tootsies will be toasty in no time.

The Bed

As with the rest of your bedroom, make your bed inviting. I like the look of a bed you can sink into like a cloud. You might prefer the crisp, more tailored look. Whatever you choose, it should say "sleep."

If you're buying a new mattress, make sure you have the option of bringing it back after you try it out. Five minutes in the showroom is not enough; anything is comfortable for five minutes. My husband and I prefer different degrees of firmness, so we purchased an air-filled mattress that can be adjusted on each side to suit the sleeper. I have a friend whose husband wakes her up tossing and turning, so she purchased a mattress that absorbs motion. If you have such special needs, shop carefully.

Take good care of your mattress. Every four to six months, flip *and* rotate it to even out wear. Kill germs with a disinfectant spray, then vacuum top and sides with the upholstery attachment. Also vacuum the box spring to eliminate all the allergens and dust mites. This should take about twenty minutes.

The Right Way to Make a Bed

Start with a mattress pad or cover; this protects the mattress from wear, and it feels more comfortable than lying down on a bare sheet and feeling mattress buttons through it. A mattress pad also protects the mattress from light stains. If you need to guard against heavier stains or spills, choose a waterproof one. If your sheets are large enough, add a downy pad or coverlet before you put the bottom sheet on; it softens and protects the mattress surface even further.

Tip: If troubled by allergies, use a polyester pillow instead of feather, and encase it in a non-allergenic plastic cover.

Next comes the bottom, fitted, or contour sheet. Place it print-side up. Stretch opposite corners on first, then fit the remaining two. Pull it snug for wrinkle-free sleeping. Some people prefer to use unelasticized flat sheets for both tops and bottoms—if so, you need to tuck in the bottom sheet very snugly so it won't sneak out of place as you sleep.

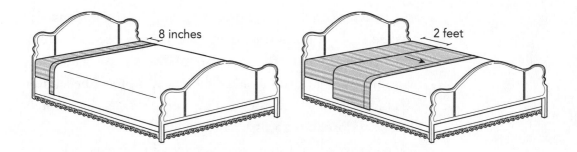

To make it easier to center the top sheet, always fold it lengthwise down the middle before storing; that way the fold serves as a guide (and the same is true for oblong tablecloths).

The top sheet should be placed with the printed side down. This is so that when you get in, and when you turn your bed back, you can see the print, or the "right" side. Tuck in the bottom end, so that the top (the part with the widest hem) rests about eight inches away from the headboard. Now tuck in the sides, as far up as you wish. To make neat hospital corners, pull up the side of the sheet about two feet from the end, and rest it on top of the mattress. This will make a triangle, and you'll tuck the bottom half of that triangle under the mattress. Now fold the sheet back down. Some people tuck it in yet again; others find this too tight for their toes.

Follow the top sheet with a blanket, tucked in, and a final cover, adding more blankets if necessary during cold weather. The final cover can be a quilt, a comforter, a bed spread, or even a beautiful tablecloth. Be creative. If your spread or comforter doesn't come down to the floor, you'll want to place a coordinating dust ruffle under

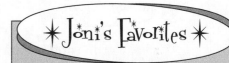

✳ Joni's Favorites ✳

My top choices for linens are Belora and Partesi, but they are hard to find—look for any high thread-count sheet that feels buttery soft.

your mattress, to hide the bottom half of the bed and give it a finished look. You can use duvet covers to enclose comforters, and switch them for different seasonal looks. I have a medium-weight down comforter inside a duvet cover on my bed, and it feels heavenly to me. If you perspire when you sleep, you might want to choose something lighter.

A good friend of mine once owned a fine linens store, and showed me the easiest way to insert a comforter into a duvet. You grab the bottom corners of the comforter, and stuff them into the bottom corners of the duvet. This takes about thirty seconds. Don't try to shake the comforter in, or let it "fall" in—you'll be wrestling your linens for half an hour.

The sides of a blanket are its most important part—this is the section that keeps drafts out and warmth in. Make sure your blanket is wide enough to hang down the sides and keep you warm.

Thicker bedspreads or comforters make it faster and easier to make a bed—they hardly wrinkle, whereas a thinner covering, such as chenille, will take more time and accuracy. But choose the look you like. And whether you fold your bedspread down at night, or use it for warmth, is a matter of personal taste.

I recommend *not* having an electric blanket. They're easy to leave on by accident, and they have caused numerous house fires. If you're cold, turn up the thermostat or add another blanket.

Last of all, finish your bed with pillows. A comfortable sleeping pillow is essential, and ideally it should be encased in a zippered pillow cover *under* the pillow case. You may want to add decorative shams and throw pillows as well (just remember they'll add to your bed-making time—and where will you store them at night?). Some people like to walk in and see a turned-down bed, all ready to climb into. If you like this idea, turn it down when you make it in the morning and smoothly tuck in the turned-down part. It will still look neatly made, but just that much more inviting.

In the morning, throw back the covers while you're getting ready for the day, to let it air and freshen. Make sure you have good ventilation in your room. Then make your bed before leaving.

Headboard Ideas

Many beds come with headboards, but if you need to design one yourself, there are many clever ways to do it. Here are a few ideas:

1. Create the look of posts by hanging a curtain panel above each corner of the bed, ceiling to floor.

2. Upholster an old or chipped headboard (or a rectangle of plywood) by wrapping with batting, then covering with fabric and trim, using a staple gun and fabric glue.

3. Use an old garden gate (or section of fence) for a twin bed headboard. Paint with flowers or wrap with silk vines. You can do the same thing with some wooden lattice from the hardware store's garden department. Another variation: top the fence with birdhouses.

4. Hang a tapestry or quilt behind your bed.

5. Put a tall bookcase behind your bed.

6. Search flea markets and architectural "bone yards" for interesting mantels, moldings, and tin ceiling panels.

7. Use a giant paper fan for a headboard.

8. Paste on a wallpaper border in the shape of a headboard.

9. Faux paint a headboard on the wall that looks like wood, marble, you name it.

10. Place an aquarium behind your bed.

11. Drape a fabric swag on the wall behind your bed. Let the ends hang down, held by decorative hardware.

12. Hang a giant wreath, or a swag of silk flowers, above your bed (and dust it frequently).

13. Hang a dowel horizontally, then sew fabric loops onto square throw pillows, and hang them from the dowel. This works great with bright colors; it looks like a row of nautical flags.

14. Create a canopy effect with wallpaper or fabric—run it up the wall behind your bed, and onto the ceiling about halfway out over the bed. Trim with molding.

15. Place a folding Japanese screen behind your bed.

16. Stencil a border on the wall that outlines where a headboard would be. Consider lettering a sleepy-time phrase on the wall.

17. Hang a kimono or other costume on the wall behind your bed.

Other Bedroom Furniture

Most people have somewhere, other than the bed, to sit and put on their stockings or whatever. Depending on your taste and the size of your room, you might choose a hassock, a trunk, a rocking chair, or an overstuffed wing back. If you're cramped for storage space, a trunk or a lidded bench is a good idea. (Don't sit on a corner of the bed; over time it will begin to droop.)

You'll need a nightstand for your alarm clock, a phone if you so choose, and a small bedside lamp (in case you like to read to get sleepy). Framed photos and other pretty objects will depend upon how large your table is.

A dresser is generally placed against one wall, often with a mirror above it. Even if you have a mirror such as this, install a full-length mirror somewhere (inside a closet door, perhaps) so you can see how you look head-to-toe, not just from the waist up.

Tip If your bed slats tend to slip, place rubber bands on the ends for traction.

If you have bare floors, a rug next to your bed makes it easier for warm feet to greet the day. Keep a robe and slippers handy.

Knickknacks, paintings, and other decorations are all fine; just make sure they are soothing. Do you really want to stay up all night watching the eyes of a Felix-the-Cat clock looking back and forth all night?

What *Not* to Put in the Bedroom

Sleep is the primary function of the bedroom, not desk work, not Internet browsing, not exercising. If you have the space, keep your work, entertainment, fitness area, and computer elsewhere, not where you need to feel drowsy. Staring at a "to-do" pile increases stress; it doesn't reduce it. You want your brain to associate this room with winding down.

People have varying opinions about television in the bedroom. I've always found it unromantic and annoying (isn't there *somewhere* we can escape from the media barrage?), but if you're a late-night TV fan, suit yourself. A good place to install a television is in an armoire where you can close the doors and have a restful-looking bedroom when not watching.

A bookcase is fine, if you have room, but not if you stay awake studying the spines and wondering what to read next. And keep hobbies, calendars, bulletin boards, briefcases, stacks of mail, and all awake-time paraphernalia in other rooms.

Do not pile laundry or dry cleaning in the bedroom; keep it in the closet where you won't see it. Another reason to keep this, and other unnecessary items, out of the bedroom is so you won't trip over them en route to the bathroom late at night.

Plants are fine, but remember that molds grow in moist soil, and you may find that you react to them.

Basically, the fewer stimuli you have in the bedroom, the more restful it will be, and the more conducive it will be to sleeping . . . as well as, of course, romance.

Chapter Thirteen

Kitchen

People love to congregate in a kitchen. It's where we feel homey, where we bask in the comfortable smells of nourishment and hospitality. It's usually bright and welcoming and more casual than a formal living room. Be sure to keep snacks and fresh fruit on hand for drop-in guests, and always offer visitors something to drink—water and ice at the very least.

Since you prepare food here, this is the one room you should keep organized and spotless, for the sake of health and safety. You'll enjoy many hours in your kitchen if you keep it shining and well maintained.

The Sponge vs. Cloth Debate

How long can you use a sponge before it's too dirty and has to be discarded? I'll tell you: about ten minutes. Okay, maybe that's an exaggeration, but sponges are notorious for harboring bacteria and smearing them on the counters that you think you're wiping clean. They may be perfect for cleaning cars and other items, but where food is concerned, I prefer a clean dish cloth each day. Air circulates in cloths better to keep germs at bay, and they're easy to toss in the hamper. (Frankly, I like paper towels better still, as you can wipe up messes and throw them away.)

For handwashing dishes, I like Palmolive dish washing soap.

If you're determined to use a sponge, at least remember to disinfect it each day by pre-soaking it in a diluted bleach mixture, or by microwaving a damp sponge for one minute on high. Tossing it into the dishwasher does not get it hot enough to kill all the bacteria.

Above all, do not use the same cleaning towels or cloths on the counter as you use on the floor. And don't use dish towels for drying hands; they'll stay cleaner if you use them only for drying clean dishes.

Walls and Doors

When you clean your kitchen, start by looking up. Are there light fixtures that need dusting or shining? Grease splatters on the ceiling or walls? Get out your cleaning tote and take care of those items first.

Now glance down a foot or two and see how the cabinets look. Wipe the doors free of grease and fingerprints. I usually use an all-purpose cleaner for this. Now open them and check for dust or debris on the shelves. Especially where you store pantry items, lift food items out and wipe under them as necessary. I always line shelves and drawers before filling them, and this makes cleanup much easier. I like to use contact paper or wallpaper, but some people like stick-on tiles or linoleum in their cupboards, especially under the sink, for quick, slick cleanups. If you have delicate china or crystal, look for thick, spongy shelf liners that will protect your treasures from hard surfaces.

If you're storing powdery items such as flour, I suggest keeping them in plastic containers with tight-fitting lids. This prevents grit from accumulating on the shelf, and it keeps pests out.

If you find you need to stack items two or three deep, elevate the back rows on blocks of wood, so you can see what you have.

Before we leave the doors and drawers, check handles for any dried-on particles, and wipe them clean with disinfectant.

Continue from top to bottom, and check the walls for food splatters, smudges, and fingerprints, especially around light switches and door knobs. Clean range hoods and microwave ovens, inside and out.

Tip: Remove crayon marks from walls with WD-40, followed by household cleaner. Or try a prewash laundry stain remover.

Finally, dust off any picture frames or ornamental objects on the walls, and using a cloth sprayed with dusting polish, wipe down any wooden furniture, such as tables and chairs that may be in your kitchen.

Counters

Using a disinfectant cleaner, wipe down the fronts of all appliances—oven and refrigerator doors and any small appliances sitting on the counter (a toothbrush helps get around small grooves and crannies)—and wash out any baskets or bowls you have on display. Run a blender with soapy water to clean it, then rinse. Do not immerse any part of an electrical appliance in water, and check owner's manuals before cleaning.

Listen to Your Mother!

The kitchen is the prime target area for pest problems. But you can head them off by keeping your kitchen as clean as possible. As mentioned above, store foodstuffs in airtight containers, and never leave crumbs, spills, or dirty dishes until morning. Another way to keep weevils and other critters out of your flour and packaged grains is to store them in the freezer (many products are infested at the supermarket and you bring them home inadvertently).

Cockroaches are a problem that can beset even the most fastidious housekeeper (especially in apartments, where they seem to move from one unit to the next). Catnip will repel them, but to kill an infestation, use boric acid compound. This will also take care of silverfish. Follow instructions carefully and keep this pesticide away from kids and pets.

Boiling water poured onto ant hills should rid you of ants, if only temporarily. Even the best exterminators will tell you that a new colony of ants can always start construction, even if you think you've scoured the area. You can repel ants by sprinkling salt or flour in their path.

Mice and rodents are able to squeeze through extremely small openings (a quarter of an inch, in some cases), so make sure there are no gaping holes around plumbing or wiring, especially under your sink and large appliances. Additionally, check the outside walls of your home or apartment, and plug any holes mice could use. Mothballs will also repel mice and squirrels.

Flies and wasps get in occasionally. Hairspray will immobilize their wings until you can swat them. Keep doors and windows screened or closed, and in the case of flies, keep garbage covered and pet droppings picked up.

Pick everything up and wipe under it to clean the counters. And don't forget to wipe down the backsplash behind your counters. The dirtiest place in most kitchens is the can-opener blade. I run mine through the dishwasher after each use, just as if it were a knife.

If your counters are stained, try scrubbing with a paste made from baking soda and lemon juice.

The Oven

Remove the burner grids and control knobs from your stove and soak them in hot, soapy water. Wipe down the top of the stove and the back where the clock and buttons are. After the grids and knobs have soaked, they'll be easier to wash. Then dry and replace them.

If your oven needs cleaning, and yours is not a self-cleaning model, spray it the night before with oven cleaner, and let it set overnight. You can soak the grates, drip pans, and hood filter overnight in a sink of soapy water, too, or just run them through the dishwasher.

> **Tip**
> An overnight oven cleaner: Leave a cup of ammonia in a closed oven. The next morning, air out the fumes and the walls should easily scrub clean.

Never line your oven with aluminum foil; you risk carbon monoxide gas poisoning. If you're concerned about drips, place a strip of foil or a cookie sheet on the lowest rack, under whatever you're baking. If you should get spills or splatters, sprinkle them with salt for a quicker cleanup once the oven cools.

To degunk a broiler pan, sprinkle it with laundry detergent, and let it set. Other pots and pans with crusty food spots can be sprinkled with baking soda and water, then left to soak for a few hours.

The Refrigerator

If you keep up with spills and crumbs that accumulate in your refrigerator (and throw out those limp veggies!), you won't have a big interior fridge cleanup. But if you've ignored a bit of grime here and there, you'll need to empty the fridge, wipe down the walls and racks, and soak the crispers in suds. Use a toothbrush to get particles out of the gaskets, the rubber seals around the door.

Now take a minute to check the foods before you put them back—is everything fresh? Do you need to wipe gunk from any jar lids? If something was sitting in a spill, clean the bottom thoroughly before putting it back again. Follow the same strategy with your freezer.

Tip: After washing the refrigerator drip pan, spray it with a diluted bleach solution to kill germs. Air dry and put back.

I keep rigid plastic containers, such as ice cube bins, in my fridge to consolidate condiments, especially for making quick sandwiches. I lift out one plastic box, and there's the mayonnaise, the cheese, the lunch meat, the mustard—all in one convenient holder. I've done the same with fresh vegetable snacks, pudding and yogurt selections, jams and jellies, and salsas. And, if any of these should spill, the spill is confined to the container, instead of dripping from one shelf to the next.

To control odors inside the fridge, place an open box of baking soda on one of the shelves (this is also a handy fire extinguisher if you should have a grease fire). Other good deodorizers are an open container of activated charcoal or a cotton ball soaked in vanilla.

Be sure to dust the top of the refrigerator, too. It's an easy spot to overlook if you can't see it at eye level. Sweep or vacuum under and behind the refrigerator, then once or twice a year you should unplug your fridge and vacuum the coils with the crevice tool attachment.

Tip

Rubber gloves are great for removing stuck jar lids.

The Dishwasher

Dishwashers can turn brown inside, but they'll sparkle immediately if you run them empty on a cycle with a little citric acid. You can find this in powdered form at the supermarket, and you'll only need a spoonful or two.

To keep utensils from falling through the utensil rack, line it with plastic mesh; water will still drain out, but handles and knife tips will stay put.

When loading your dishwasher, keep in mind the direction of the water spray, and let dishes face center. Don't put larger pots and bowls on the bottom rack, even if they can withstand the heat—their size will block the water from reaching items on the top rack. If

Joni's Favorites

For dishwashing detergent, I prefer Cascade.

your larger bowls won't fit on the top rack, hand wash them.

Never wash sterling silver or silver plate items in a dishwasher; you'll ruin the finish. Wash these (and china and crystal) by hand.

The Sink

Baking soda is a wonderful cleaner for most sinks, and it's great for pouring into the drain to control odors. Rust marks are often a problem in sinks. If your sink is porcelain, use a wet scrub brush and cream of tartar to remove rust. If it's stainless steel, a touch of lighter fluid will do the trick. Stainless steel also cleans up well with rubbing alcohol, club soda, or white vinegar. If your sink is clogged, try pouring baking powder down the drain, followed by boiling water. And never put stringy food items, such as onions or celery, down the disposal.

Tip: **If your disposal won't turn on, look at the unit under your sink, and press the red reset button.**

Let your disposal grind up orange or lemon peels for a fresh citrus scent. Don't forget to polish the faucet and handles.

Cutting Boards

Here's another debate for you. Every year or so, experts advocate wooden ones, then plastic ones. I'll tell you the real key to cutting boards: choose whichever one you want, but disinfect it every time you use it. Scratches, whether in wood or plastic, trap germs, but a simple spritz of very diluted bleach takes care of it. I also recommend having separate boards for cutting meats and for vegetables, so you don't risk getting meat proteins on your fresh produce.

To keep your cutting board from sliding around as you use it, place a damp dish towel, or a mouse pad, under it. Mouse pads are great under mixing bowls, too, to keep them in place.

The Kitchen Floor

If you've been cleaning right, you'll have wiped lots of crumbs and junk onto the floor as you've cleaned, and this is the last spot that will need attention before you can step back and proudly view your sparkling kitchen. I like to vacuum, then mop to rid the kitchen floor of all debris.

If your floor is wood, only use cleaners specified for wood floors. If it's linoleum, you can make a terrific cleaner by mixing ½ cup bleach, ¼ cup vinegar, and 1 gallon of hot water.

Trash It!

Wash out your kitchen wastebasket and spray it with disinfectant before relining with a plastic trash bag. If you use a trash compactor, vacuum out crumbs and glass chips with a hand-held vacuum, then wipe up with a disinfectant cleaner.

Tip

Run ice cubes and egg shells through your disposal to sharpen the blades.

If dogs tend to tear into your outside garbage, spray cans with ammonia to keep them at a distance. And always use trash cans with lids you can clamp on tightly. This prevents having your trash strewn around (a yucky cleanup job if there ever was one—wear disposable plastic gloves), and it also keeps rodents from moving in.

Now, launder and replace any rugs or mats, and you're done!

Equipping Your Kitchen

Here is a basic list of all the utensils, cutlery, pots and pans, and dishes you'll need in your kitchen. You can get by with less, but if you do a moderate amount of cooking and baking, you will probably need all these things at some point. Of course, what you see as a necessary kitchen item depends on what you like to prepare: some people find a lemon zester indispensable, others never see the need for one.

For myself, a good pair of kitchen scissors is my number one kitchen tool. I use my scissors instead of a knife for many things; they're great for preparing salads, cutting meat, and so on. And you can run them through the dishwasher to keep clean. My next most important kitchen tool is a good set of knives. You can spend a lot of money on a well-made set, which often includes scissors, and you should choose the best you can afford. Avoid buying a cheap set of a dozen knives you'll never use. The basics are a paring knife, a utility knife, a chef's knife, and a serrated bread knife. I like using a large butcher knife for mincing and many other uses, but if you're hesitant to use one, don't buy one.

Here are the basics of a well-stocked kitchen:

A good set of knives, including scissors

A pizza cutter (also great for slicing sandwiches, quesadillas, and more)

> **Tip**
> Rub Vaseline around screw-on lids that tend to stick, such as tubes of glue.

Two cutting boards

A set of cooking pots—including a soup pot, smaller sauce pans, a large and a small frying pan, and a roasting pan

Dishes, bowls, and glasses for at least four, ideally twelve

A set of utensils for the same

A drawer organizer for utensils

A juice pitcher

A set of mixing bowls

Measuring cups and spoons

Baking pans: two cake pans, two pie plates, two loaf pans, and a muffin tin

A rolling pin

A sifter

A strainer

A timer

A baster

A pasta fork

Tongs

An electric mixer

Two or three platters or trays

Two cookie sheets

A cooling rack (or use an oven rack)

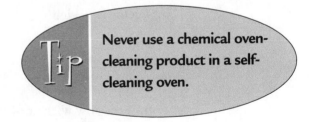

Tip

Never use a chemical oven-cleaning product in a self-cleaning oven.

Three or four microwave-safe baking dishes (for casseroles)

Two metal baking pans (nine by thirteen inch)

A set of steak knives

A fruit and vegetable scrub brush

A soup ladle

Five large serving spoons

Two slotted spoons

Three wooden spoons

Three rubber spatulas or scrapers

Three pancake-turner spatulas

An ice cream scoop (after all, ice cream is important)

A can opener

A bottle opener

A vegetable peeler

A wire whisk

A meat thermometer

A grater (spray with cooking spray before using for faster cleanup)

A colander

Plastic wrap

Aluminum foil

Resealable plastic bags

Paper towels

Napkins

Several rigid, lidded plastic containers for storing food in the fridge

Two or three trivets, to protect your table from hot serving dishes

A bread basket (line with a linen towel, and wrap rolls or breads to keep them warm)

Four potholders or oven mitts

Six dish towels, at least

Ten dishcloths

Assorted cleaning rags (but keep them out of view)

A dish-draining rack

Vases and other containers for flowers

Candlesticks and candles

Matches

A fire extinguisher

A good, basic cookbook (Try my other book in this series, *Cooking Secrets My Mother Never Taught Me*.)

Putting Everything Away

Take plenty of time to organize your kitchen. Most people organize things the way their parents did, but don't just mindlessly load your cabinets. Every kitchen (and every cook) is different; you need to establish your own system. Really think before you put each item away and ask yourself these questions:

Do I really use this? (If not, discard.)

Where do I use it? (If it's a pancake turner, store it by the stove where you make pancakes. If plates, store them close to where you eat. Store everything where you use it. You'll save steps by placing everything in the most convenient spot.)

Does this item need to be placed with similar items in an organizer? (If so, buy the organizers and put things away properly.)

> **Tip**
> Occasionally a plastic bread bag or other wrapper will melt onto a hot appliance, such as a toaster. You can remove it with Vaseline.

Are the things I use most often closest to my fingertips? (I probably use my scissors every day, so I keep them in the most accessible drawer.)

Can I access way in the back of high cabinets? (If not, consider roll-out bins.)

If something is sitting out (such as a crock of spoons and spatulas), will I use them often enough to keep them clean? (The same applies to hanging pots and pans.)

If there are children in the house, are unbreakable cups and bowls accessible to them? (Kids can help themselves, and you'll save having to reach up for them all the time.)

To keep knives sharp, don't just pile them in a drawer. It's also dangerous if you reach in and hit a blade. Keep them mounted on a magnetized strip on the wall, or store them blade-side-up in a knife block.

A clever place to store drinking glasses is in the refrigerator door, if you have the space. Then the glasses are chilled and ready. I keep some thick ice cream goblets in the freezer for this same purpose.

Be sure to utilize the surface inside cupboard doors, too. These are great places for hanging spice charts, calendars, dish towels, and lunch bags.

The Proper Way to Set a Table

This is a slam dunk. First, set out either a tablecloth or place-mats. If using a tablecloth, I like to put a felt pad underneath it. Place the dinner plate about half an inch from the edge of the table. To its immediate right goes the knife, blade facing inward. Next to the knife is a spoon, and if you're using a soup spoon, you can either place it third in line on the right, or above the plate, horizontally. The drinking glass and wine glass, if used, also go on the right, just above the knife.

To the left of the plate are the forks and the napkin. You may place the napkin under or to the left of the forks. If serving guests, cloth napkins are a nice touch; fold them, tuck them into a napkin ring, or tie them with a pretty bow.

On the far left is the salad fork, since you'll use that first. Then, next to the plate itself, is the larger dinner fork. If using a bread plate, it goes on the left, above the forks. A salad plate goes immediately to the left of the forks.

We can get more complicated; if you're serving appetizers or shellfish, you'll use additional plates and special utensils. But for most meals, the above table setting will do just fine. Be sure to set out butter and a butter knife on a butter dish or small plate, and make salt and pepper accessible to those who want them.

I always feel a table looks better with a centerpiece or candles, or both. Even if you're eating all alone, light the candles, put on some music, and make dining special.

After the meal, wrap and refrigerate leftovers; a good rule of thumb is that anything left at room temperature for two hours or more could spoil and must be discarded.

Clearing the table can be made easier in a couple of ways. For informal family meals, you can load dirty dishes into a dish pan to save yourself trips, or roll them away on a rolling cart.

I prefer not to stack dirty dishes, however. If you keep the backs clean, you'll save rinsing time. Even if it means making a few trips back and forth, I'd rather carry the plates individually. And never scrape dishes at the dinner table, piling all the scraps onto one plate. Scraping should be done at the sink or garbage area.

Chapter Fourteen

The Big Entrance

The entryway to your home is one of its most important parts. Not only does it give visitors a first and last impression, but it affects how *you* feel as you come in the door. You want your entryway to express your personality, to feel welcoming, and to be neat and clean. In other words, here is where you put your best foot forward.

First and Last Impressions

Let's start with the outside. Keep the area by your front door swept and tidy. This is easier to do if you live in an apartment. Brush away leaves and cobwebs, shake the dirt out of your doormat, and make sure your bell or buzzer is clean and working. If you own a home, that neatness extends right to the curb and includes many more chores and gardening efforts.

But yard and garden care could be its own book. For now, we'll focus on the porch and entryway itself.

163

The Porch

Stand outside your door and pretend you're just seeing it for the first time. What's the impression? If you want anonymity, simply keep the area swept. But if you want a little creativity, and the sense of a cared-for home, you'll want to add your own touches—a door hanging or wreath, pretty address or door numbers, a welcome mat, a potted plant, or maybe even a bench (bolted down, in this day and age, so it won't "walk" off).

Don't crowd a small porch with a thousand doo-dads, but if you have room, you can create a seasonal display or at least some pots with healthy, seasonal plants growing in them. Consider the roofline; does it overhang to protect plants from rain and snow? Or, if you *want* rainfall, are your plants placed where they can receive it? Look through garden magazines and nurseries for unusual planters, mailboxes, rocks, birdhouses, bells, wrought-iron sculptures, antique sleds or wagons, and other outdoor decorations.

There are hundreds of beautiful doormats available, but if you have problems with mud or snow tracking in, get a sturdy, bushy doormat that will really do the job.

If windows are visible from your porch, be sure to keep them clean, and close draperies or blinds for privacy (or if you don't mind visitors looking in, open them).

Make sure your porch light is clean and working. It's not only a welcoming gesture to leave a light on, but a safety essential if you come in after dark.

The Front Door

If you own your own home, you might want to consider updating the front door itself. The front door has a considerable impact on the overall exterior appearance. Perhaps it's time for a new coat of paint, a stain, or a completely new replacement. Consider a bright white door, a red one, a yellow one—something with drama and life, especially if the rest of your home is gray or brick.

Wreaths

Your front door (or the wall near it) will probably look more welcoming with something hanging there to please the eye. It doesn't have to be a wreath; you can adorn your porch with a swag, a bunch of sprigs tied with a bow, a holiday figure, a half-basket, a string of chili peppers, or just about anything.

First of all, make sure your decoration contrasts with the door itself. I once brought home a beautiful grapevine wreath—or so I thought, until it camouflaged itself perfectly against my brown door! (In that house, I learned to use white or light-colored wreaths so they'd show up.) And, if you have double doors, get two.

> **Tip**
> A bow or ribbon can dress up even the simplest wreath. Leave two ribbon ends hanging, and cut them into inverted V-shapes.

Next, consider the size of your ornament. You don't want to overwhelm the house with a gigantic wreath as large as the door itself. Smaller and simpler is usually best.

Decide how you'll hang your wreath—do you want to hammer a nail into your door? Will your landlord make you replace the door if you do? There are many wreath hangers available that do not mar your door; they come in brass, black, white, and other colors. These fit over the top of the door, then fold down with an L-shaped hook to hold the wreath.

Listen to Your Mother!

Besides the classic, round wreath, here are some other artistic options for your door:

Wrap a rectangular picture frame with greenery to create a novel shape. Tie a bunch of lavender to each side, or adorn it with anything you like.

Hang shiny Christmas balls from ribbons.

Tie a row of dried flower bouquets from a horizontal twig.

Hang a pretty plate from a ribbon.

Tie a bow around a straw hat, and hang it on your door.

Hang a flag on your door.

Nestle small terra cotta pots in a wreath tied with ivy.

Use fluffy hydrangeas or big magnolias in a large wreath.

Hang a brass horn with a satin cord.

Hang a friendly mask.

Tie a bunch of Indian corn with a raffia bow.

Hang bells that ring when the door opens.

Post a wooden plaque with a welcoming message painted on it.

Glue treasures onto a purchased wreath (sea shells, buttons, beads, cookie cutters, artificial sprigs of nuts and dried berries). Leave it natural or spray gold.

Make a heart-shaped wreath (fashion a primitive one by bending willow twigs into a loop, and tying it to another loop).

Display a birdhouse.

Nestle an inexpensive doll in a wreath, as if she's sitting on a swing.

Hang a sailboat, a rocking horse, or some other "antique" on your door.

Change the decoration seasonally if you like. Store unused wreaths by hanging them in a garage or other storage area, and cover them with a trash bag to shield them from dust. Don't lay them flat or they'll be more likely to get crushed under something else.

The Entrance

Now let's step inside. Whether you have an actual foyer or not, you can establish an "entry" feeling by the way you arrange furniture. The entryway can be defined by a coat rack, a banister or railing, potted plants, a small table, a low bookcase, an aquarium, art objects, just about anything. My husband collects canes, and we have an antique cane/umbrella stand by the front door. Sometimes you can pave a small space with tiles or marble to define an entrance.

Again, look up and check the lighting—is it bright enough? Dressy enough? Too fussy? Too blah? Get a fixture you really love, and that goes with the rest of your things. (If your fixture hangs from a chain, consider wrapping a ribbon or a silk floral vine around the chain.)

Mirrors are wonderful for making areas look larger, and for reflecting the pretty objects you own. Consider paintings, vases, and interesting boxes that can define your entryway, too.

When you first step in, you should have somewhere to put things down—shopping bags, your purse, keys, mail, whatever. So it's good to have a nearby table with some clear space for your armloads. I like something scented on the table, too, so when you walk in, it's a treat for all your senses. Scented candles have been getting bad publicity for releasing lead into the air if they have metal in their wicks, so make sure yours don't, or contact the manufacturer to see if they used lead. Other options are a bowl of potpourri or fresh flowers.

✴ **Joni's Favorites** ✴

I like a rug just inside the door—not only does it soften the feel of the entryway, but it collects a little more dust that your doormat missed and keeps your home cleaner.

If you don't have a coat closet, some Shaker pegs or a free-standing coat rack provide a convenient place to stow jackets and hats. A friend of mine painted a mural of a hat rack loaded with hats, right on the wall; it's so realistic it makes you want to hang your hat there!

Displays

Something you might consider just inside your doorway is a display of collectibles, or a seasonal arrangement on a hutch or table. It's fun to mark the holidays with items you might not otherwise display. (After all, how many times can you use that gorgeous Thanksgiving platter?) Visitors enjoy a change of scenery, and look forward to seeing your next collection. Here are some display ideas to brighten up your entry.

✳ **January:** Snowmen. Let friends know you're collecting them, and you'll soon have enough for an entire snow village! Scatter feathery snow crystals around. Or, create a New Year's display with confetti and streamers.

✳ **February:** Valentine's. A book of love poems, a satin candy box, treasured keepsake Valentines, a bowl of conversation hearts, heart-shaped anything. Ribbons and bows. A teacup filled with roses.

✳ **March/April:** An Easter or Springtime collection—a topiary with a bird's nest tucked in it, colorful eggs, bunnies, baskets, candies. Or, St. Patrick's Day with green shamrocks and a bucket of gilded chocolate coins.

✳ **May/June:** Gardening—a painted watering can, decorative garden gloves and tools, pretty seed packets, potted flowers, a pretty coffeetable book about gardening.

* **July:** Fourth of July. Americana. Flags and patriotism.

* **August:** Summertime. Strawberries. Watermelon. Honey bees and beehives. A picnic basket with a red-and-white-checkered cloth. Tiny wooden adirondack chairs, sunflowers, nautical sailing-themed anything, seashells, a beach bucket. A friend of mine surrounded a wall mirror with a collection of children's Japanese sandals.

* **September:** Autumn. Baskets of apples, pretty colored leaves, nuts and seeds, golden chrysanthemums, a charming old felt hat.

Listen to Your Mother!

What do you do if you suddenly have guests and the place is a mess? If you've been keeping up with the cleaning, drop-in guests should be no problem. But we all get caught now and then with our dust bunnies down, so here are some tricks to whip your home into shape when you only have a few minutes:

Utilize oven and dishwasher space—quickly store kitchen items out of sight. Just be sure you remember to take them out before you turn on the appliances!

Make shiny things shine—clean fingerprints from mirrors and countertops. Use baby wipes for a quick shine on faucets.

Gather up living room clutter in a bag or basket, and store it in the bedroom.

Spritz room spray.

Turn on pleasant music.

Rub down upholstered furniture with a rubber glove to remove pet hair.

Fluff and straighten pillows.

Open the door, smile, and, if you're a woman, hope you're wearing a bra.

✴ **October:** Halloween with ghosts, scarecrows, jack-o-lanterns, black cats, and bats. Or, go the harvest route with gourds, pumpkins, wheat, Indian corn, and dried flowers.

✴ **November:** Keep the harvest items, and add pilgrims and Indians or a whimsical turkey.

✴ **December:** Create a knockout Christmas or Hanukkah display. There are so many options for these holidays, I'm sure you won't lack for ideas. Think about nutcracker collections, menorahs, Santa displays, even ribbons bejeweled with ornaments or swags of greenery festooned with fruit. Angels, Christmas books, a nativity scene, gold and silver objects, Santa's workshop with toys, Christmas pillows—the list is endless.

And of course, pretty china, flowers, and seasonal photos are always lovely. Scout around your home for trinkets and treasures that could work their way into a fun display. Check fabric stores for yardage printed with seasonal designs that you can use *under* your collections.

Part Four

Wrapping It Up

Chapter Fifteen

A Safe Haven

You can clean it until it sparkles, and decorate it until it's drop-dead gorgeous, but if your home isn't safe, you'd better not live there just yet. Making your home safe and preparing for emergencies is not only common sense; it's the key to peace of mind when you go to bed at night.

Home Security

Prevent break-ins by making your home an unattractive target to burglars. First, keep your home well lit. Burglars would rather pick on a dark house where they can work unseen. I like the motion detector lights that flip on whenever anyone approaches.

Next, don't offer additional hiding spots for burglars by letting shrubs get overgrown. Keep bushes trimmed back to expose possible intruders.

Install dead-bolt locks. They're inexpensive and highly recommended as a deterrent to thieves. However, if you have children, make sure they know how to use them properly, should they need to exit during a fire, for example.

Get a dog with a good, loud bark. Burglars would rather try a quiet home than one where they might be attacked, or where owners are alerted by the barking.

Make it look as if you're home. At night, have lights come on randomly (not all at once), as if you're moving from room to room. There are many timers that can do this. In the day-

Listen to Your Mother!

Every home should have a first-aid kit, logically stored in the kitchen or bathroom (or both) where most accidents occur. I keep mine in a lidded plastic bin, and include sunscreens and common cold medications as well. I also keep a package of frozen veggies in the freezer—these make a moldable ice pack perfect for applying quickly to injuries (small vegetables such as corn and peas are best).

Here are the basics you should have in your first-aid box:

A first-aid booklet, if you aren't trained;

Hydrogen peroxide, to dab on cuts to prevent infection;

Rubbing alcohol, to sterilize and kill bacteria;

Cotton balls, for dabbing on the hydrogen peroxide;

Band Aids. Skip the dots and teensy strips; have a supply of regular and large bandages;

Triple antibiotic cream. Apply to cuts and burns before covering with a bandage, to ward off infection;

Sterile gauze and tape, for bigger wounds and scrapes;

Scissors, for cutting gauze and tape; and,

Medication for pain and reducing fever, such as aspirin, Tylenol, and so on.

light, burglars are often deterred if it appears that workmen are coming and going—you don't want to leave a ladder out all the time, but on occasion it doesn't hurt to leave out a lawn-mower or tools that indicate you'll be coming right back. (Of course, depending on your neighborhood, you could also get your lawnmower and ladder stolen!)

Put obstacles in the way of a quick escape. Park your car in the drive so it would be harder for thieves to pull up. On trash day, place your cans so you know how to get around them, but strangers might have a tougher time navigating. If you don't object to gates and fences, those also pose one more barrier for thieves to climb over.

Switch any hollow-core doors, which kick open easily, to solid-core doors, which are sturdier.

If you've recently purchased a new TV or any other valuable electronic item, don't just toss the box into your trash—cut it up and place it in another sack to conceal the label.

Consider investing in an alarm system; sometimes just having one is a deterrent, and it can also reduce insurance costs. A good alarm system will protect the perimeter of your home—if a door or window is opened, a circuit is broken and an alarm will sound. (Alert houseguests so they won't decide to open a window and enjoy the evening breeze only to find a police-man staring back at them.) Some alarms will automatically dial the police. I had one of these once, and its only draw-back was that strong winds would also set it off, thus drag-ging the police over to my house every time the wind blew—literally.

> **Tip**
> Don't keep priceless jewelry in a jewelry box. Store it with the pots and pans, or behind books in a bookcase.

Another option is an interior motion detector, though it might also detect large pets or dogs. On the other hand, if you have a large animal with large enough teeth, that could be a protection all in itself.

A security camera can be very effective (though ours got stolen); just be sure to place it higher than teenagers can climb on a stack of lawn chairs.

The bottom line with an alarm system is to shop carefully, talk to a lot of experts, and then decide if the emotional security is worth the financial cost.

Avoiding Illness

Here are the top five ways to stay healthy:

1. Wash your hands frequently. We touch germ-covered surfaces all the time, and the quickest way to catch a cold is to then rub our eyes or touch our food with these same germ-covered hands.

2. Keep your fingers out of your nose. Okay, I know I sound like your mother now, but this goes beyond the fact that picking one's nose is disgusting. You know how cocaine addicts put the drugs up their noses? This is because nasal membranes are so thin that whatever touches them goes right into the bloodstream. If you touch them with a fingertip, whammo! Bacteria and viruses get right to work. Who would have thought we could learn something from drug addicts, but there you go.

> **Tip**
> An upset stomach will be helped with ½ cup cream and ½ cup ginger ale.

3. Get your rest. If you lose a few hours of sleep in just one night, your resistance could drop, your immune system can weaken, and you'll "catch" all those germs that are already all over the place. The only reason you aren't catching them most of the time is because your body is strong and is fighting them.

4. Eat right. Take your vitamins, especially zinc for avoiding sore throats. Keep your machine running on premium fuel, not greasy garbage that can impair your immune system.

5. Avoid chills. If you do get chilled, take a hot bath or two, and wear something on your feet. Most of our body heat escapes through our head, so if it's a chilly day, wear a hat. Enjoy a bowl of hot chicken soup—it's loaded with healthy electrolytes. Take a jacket with you, just in case. Stay warm.

> **Tip**
> Rub half a lime on your forehead to cure a headache.

Emergency Supplies

No matter where you live, you're at the mercy of Mother Nature. You're also at the mercy of power outages, fires, and freak accidents that require us to pull out the survival stuff. Some people keep two stashes—a big one for emergency supplies you'd use in your home, including a pantry full of food, and then a smaller one for grab-and-run supplies, should you need to evacuate quickly for seventy-two hours or less

> **Tip**
> A dab of Crazy Glue on a scratch will hold the skin together until the healing can begin.

(ideally packed in dufflebags or backpacks that you can literally carry and run with).

I recommend establishing both kinds of emergency storage, but start with the basics and add on as you're able. Keep your items wherever you have room, but in air-tight containers if possible. Consider putting everything in grab-and-run backpacks, then storing the backpacks in a new plastic garbage can with a tight-fitting lid. By the way, you can cover this can with a wooden round and a long tablecloth to create an instant table that nobody will guess is concealing your emergency supplies. Two other good spots are under the bed and inside window seats or benches. And don't forget to keep some supplies in the trunk of your car (see chapter 9).

Some splinters can be removed by pressing with Scotch tape, then pulling off the tape.

To ease the itch of a mosquito bite, rub it with soap.

Here are the minimum supplies to have on hand should disaster strike:

A three-day supply of nonperishable food (pop-top cans of tuna and fruit, granola bars, drinks, and so on)

Bottled water (three gallons per person)

Paper plates and cups, plastic utensils

Tissue, toilet paper, tampons

Toiletry items—toothbrush, toothpaste, soap, towel, razor, comb, and so on

A roll of paper towels

Wet Wipes

Hand disinfecting liquid

Plastic bags

A sleeping bag

A flashlight

A radio

Fresh batteries for the above two

Candles and matches (regular and waterproof)

A fire extinguisher

A pair of work gloves

Extra keys

Identification

Cash in small bills and coins

Another first-aid kit, apart from the one you keep easily accessible.

Water purification tablets

A solar blanket—these come folded up in a package about the size of a small notepad

Prescription medication

A change of clothing, including a foldable rain poncho

A small tool kit, in case you need to make a repair or shut off gas or water

A small sewing kit

A list of important phone numbers

An extra, fully charged battery if you have a cell phone

Constant Safety

To maintain basic safety, install smoke and carbon monoxide detectors. A great way to remember when to replace the batteries is to do it twice a year—when daylight savings time begins and ends. Every dwelling should have several smoke alarms; one in the hallway is not enough.

Keep ABC all-purpose fire extinguishers handy, especially in the kitchen, but also know how to use them. You can't just throw the thing into the flames, after all. You must pull the pin, aim at the base of the fire, squeeze the handle, and spray back and forth until the flames are out. Fire extinguishers are for small flare-ups, not major fire-fighting. Don't wait until there's an emergency to read the instructions and practice using one. (As mentioned earlier, baking soda is also a good extinguisher to have on hand for small grease fires.)

Of all the troubleshooting you can do, electrical safety is one area to leave to the professionals. An electrician can inspect your home and check your plugs, fuses, wiring, and appliances to make sure you're safe. Otherwise, you're guessing and taking the considerable risk of, say, electrocution. So if you're in doubt about your home's electrical safety, call in an expert.

There are many things you can do to avoid electrical trouble in the first place:

✳ Unplug anything if the outlet feels warm to the touch.

✳ Don't overload an outlet.

✳ Don't use anything that has a frayed cord or exposed wiring.

✳ Place cords behind furniture where people won't trip over them.

✳ Don't block the cooling vents of appliances that can over-heat.

✳ Don't let any cords come near water.

✳ Make sure gadgets and appliances are turned off before you plug them in.

✳ Keep children and pets away from electrical cords.

✳ Always use the appropriate wattage (or lower) listed on lamp and lighting labels.

Chapter Sixteen

The Additional Responsibilities of Home Ownership

*
If you are a first-time homeowner, congratulations! You are now qualified to gripe about taxes, stare with confusion at a bank loan application, install a doggie door, and wander down the aisles of the hardware store looking weary, but wise, as you search for a one-inch washer. You have joined millions of Americans who are learning all the stuff they don't teach in school: how to manage debt, how to get along with noisy (or nosy) neighbors, how to get a phone installed, what to do if somebody falls over a sprinkler head on your property, how to install a dead-bolt lock, what kind of insurance you want, and what it feels like when a teenager runs his or her bike over your manicured lawn.

But there are numerous perks to ownership, too. You can make any improvements to your home that you want, decorate any way you like, and you stand to gain every time your property increases in value. You will also find that you have a greater connection to your immediate community. You have a vested interest in seeing that potholes get filled, trash gets emptied, gas prices stay down, and power lines stay up. You have the freedom that ownership brings and a shared sense of purpose with those around you.

However, owning a home comes with additional "housekeeping" responsibilities that extend beyond making sure the bathrooms sparkle and the rugs aren't full of cat hair. You need to keep your home, inside and out, so that it doesn't impose on or endanger others. And there are other organizational strategies that will help you keep track of your suddenly more complicated life. If you have just purchased your first home, keep these tips in mind:

1. Establish a file. Even if it's only in a cardboard box, keep records. Label each folder with the categories you need. These might include Banking (including account numbers), Receipts, Bills Paid, Contracts, Tax Records, Duplicate Records, Insurance, Mortgages, Deeds, Stocks, Medical (including eyeglass prescriptions), Home Security, Repair Estimates, Automotive, Computer, Essential Records (birth certificate, passport, and so on), Emergency Information, Legal Documents, Warranties, Instruction Booklets, Correspondence, and whole files for work-related topics, travel information, takeout menus, even coupons—and any other paperwork you need to save. *Toss*

the rest. You will never get on top of the clutter if you don't learn to throw some things away.

2. Be a good neighbor. Watch out for those who live near you, and consider hosting a Neighborhood Watch meeting. Be aware of suspicious activity. Welcome other newcomers with a plate of brownies, and notice if somebody isn't picking up the newspaper or their mail. Don't be too busy to chat on occasion and to offer help when it's needed. Besides the fact that it's courteous and friendly, being on good terms with your neighbors always pays dividends. You will need their cooperation if you want to make changes to your property that impact them, and if they are making changes that impact your property, you have already developed a base of goodwill and trust that will help resolve any difficult issues or conflicts.

3. On that subject, make sure you are not posing any hazards to others. Do not allow holes in your lawn to remain unfilled. Don't leave nails sticking out of your fence or electrical wiring exposed. Sweep up any broken glass and throw out trash lying outside. Don't have wild parties that keep the neighbors awake, and make sure your pets are not running loose and digging up your neighbors' yards. Ask yourself, "Is there anything about my property that could irritate or harm another person?"

4. Keep a calendar. This can be a Day-Timer, a wall calendar, whatever works best for you. Jot down appointments and social engagements the minute you agree to them. At the beginning of the year, fill in everybody's birthday or other events you want to remember. Block out some down time.

It's easy to fill a calendar with productive-looking notes, but to function at your best, you also need scheduled breaks.

5. Schedule yearly and biannual home maintenance. This includes turning your mattress, cleaning the chimney, winterizing pipes, checking air-conditioning and heating systems, vacuuming refrigerator coils, conducting fire drills, updating emergency supplies, cleaning the rain gutters, fertilizing plants, and putting fresh batteries in the smoke detectors.

6. Recycle. Establish separate bins and discard garbage properly. Stack and tie newspapers, crush boxes, and put them in the paper bin. Collect all aluminum in one place. Same for glass and plastic. Watch the newspaper for notices about when and where you can dispose of toxic trash.

7. Attend community/homeowner meetings. Whether it's a district meeting to decide whether to put in a stoplight on your corner, or whether your neighbors want a basketball hoop restriction, be part of the decision and make your voice heard.

8. Keep up the appearance of your home. Don't let paint peel, weeds grow, and junk accumulate. Take pride in a tidy walkway, an orderly garage, a working porch light, a neat lawn. Shovel snow from your walk, and clean up after your animals. Give your neighbors reason to be glad you live there.

9. Be prepared. If you live in an area prone to a particular natural disaster—such as earthquakes, tornadoes, or floods—take the appropriate precautions. If you live in earthquake country, bolt bookcases to the wall and don't put a bed

under a window or under shelves of breakables. If floods are common, have sandbags ready. Know where hospitals and emergency shelters are. For more on home safety, see chapter 15, "A Safe Haven."

10. Know your liabilities. If you serve alcohol, be aware that you could be sued, should an accident result.

11. Handle correspondence properly. RSVP when invitations request it. Send a condolence card or letter when someone loses a loved one (see page 188). Write thank-you notes in a timely fashion. Be gracious; it's the hallmark of a civilized society. Stock up on wedding, congratulations, thank-you cards, and such—even gifts, so you'll always have one when you need it.

12. Establish a home office space. Even if it's not a desk, you can fill a box with stamps, notepads, envelopes, paper clips, and the like and put it on the kitchen table when you need it. It will keep everything consolidated, and you'll be much more efficient at handling bills and paperwork. Keep an address book there, stationery, even wrapping paper, tape, and ribbon.

13. Get a set of tools. At the very minimum, you should own a hammer, a standard set of screwdrivers (including flat and Phillips head), wire cutters, pliers, a crescent wrench, a level, a tape measure, scissors, masking tape, packing tape, duct tape, sturdy twine, string, nails, screws, wood glue, a paint brush and paint that matches your home, lawn and garden equipment, nuts, bolts, and washers. There are also wall

Tip

Dab tools with Turtle Wax to prevent rust and keep them like new.

and crack fillers, such as Erase-a-Hole, that are great for filling in nail holes.

How to Write a Sensitive Condolence Note

Most people cringe at the thought of expressing sympathy—not because they don't feel any, but because they're afraid they'll say the wrong thing and make matters worse. And so they opt for the worst possible choice: silence.

When someone has lost a loved one, silence is by far the cruelest response. Even if you say or write something you think sounds bumbling, at least you will have expressed caring, and that caring almost always comes through. It's important to acknowledge the loss, and express your love and compassion.

Your note does not have to "make it all better." You do not have to share some profound silver lining to this tragedy, or imply that it was God's will. Simply saying that you're sorry, and you know the other person is hurting, is enough.

It's also a caring gesture to offer specific help. Don't say, "Let me know if there's anything I can do." Say, "I'm going to the theater on June 11th; I have an extra ticket—will you come?" Or, "I'd like to drop a meal by on Friday—would that be convenient?" Or, "I can watch the kids for you this weekend if you need a break," or, "I'll call tomorrow and see if you feel up to having lunch—I know a quiet cafe where we can chat." Make your offer date-specific and you're more likely to be of use.

Sometimes a hug and a whispered "I love you" will do more to heal pain than anything else you can think of. If you can't be there in person, call on the phone. Sometimes the bereaved just need to talk; it's therapeutic. They need us to share their tears and memories, to talk over their anger and confusion, to simply shore them up when they feel like collapsing. Be part of the superstructure.

There are several tactful ways to write a note—sometimes you scarcely know someone, but you want to express your caring in a card. Here are some samples you can rewrite to suit your own needs:

"I was so sorry to hear about your father. Please know that I care and I'm keeping you in my prayers."

"May you take strength from knowing you have the support of many who love and admire you."

"May God ease your burdens and comfort you with the many memories you have of your wonderful relationship."

"Words are inadequate, but please know that I'm thinking of you and wishing I could be there to hold you and share your sorrow."

"When I lost my father, I found it helpful to . . ."

"Your father was a great man. I will never forget the time (elaborate). He will be greatly missed, but I'm thankful he touched my life."

Above all, speak from your heart. These are the times when we need to drop worries about appearance and simply reach out to another soul in pain. True love vanquishes fear.

Living On Your Own for the First Time

So you are out on your own for the first time—congratulations! You will be learning about things you may not have paid much attention to before, such as: how to pick a doctor, how to seat guests at a party so a fight won't break out, and how to find a bank that offers free checking.

But you also have some perks. You can pretty much make your own schedule, your goals and successes are all within shooting range, you can hang purple towels in the bathroom if you like, and you can book an airline reservation and a hotel room. You'll have a greater interest in the community around you and more power to help others and make changes in your small section of the world.

> **Tip**
>
> Get a separate credit card for on-line purchases only. Keep its limit low so thieves won't be able to send you into debt. Then your "regular" card number stays private and protected.

Many of the tips for owning your own home may also apply to you, but here are some additional tips for when you are out on your own for the first time:

✳ Get to know the local merchants. Where's the best pizza place? Dry cleaners? Car wash? Bakery? Plug in.

✳ Be a savvy consumer. Don't give your credit card number out over the phone or the Internet. Be aware that there are scams out there, and request in writing that your name not be placed on a mailing list (many companies share lists of customers).

✳ This is optional, but I recommend keeping a scrapbook. Not only does it give you a place to preserve small items you want to save, but it displays photos and reminds us of important relationships and memories, names and dates. Be sure to use acid-free paper, so your memorabilia will last. This becomes even more important if you have children and want to document their childhoods.

So You're Moving

So many people dread moving, but they shouldn't. Moving is a grand adventure, especially if you're moving far away—you get to keep all your old friends, and make a whole bunch of new ones!

New spaces are exciting to work with, and it's another chance to organize, weed out, and get a fresh start. You can leave behind the decorating errors you made before, and make all new ones! (ha-ha.)

A wise lady once told me, when I was sad about having to move, that "if you're not green, you're not growing," and I realized that putting ourselves in new situations is good for us. It forces us to extend ourselves, learn new things, and develop new traits.

Let's start with selling your house. Realtors advise the following, to help your home sell quickly and for a higher price:

Curb appeal—What impression will people have when they first pull up and see your home? Keep your lawn green and trimmed; scatter mulch around planted flowers. Clean rain gutters, brush away cobwebs, sweep the porch and walkway. Polish hardware on your front door and wash the windows. Could the trim use a new coat of paint?

A clean interior—If ever you needed your home to be spotless, this is the time. Store clutter (emptier homes look larger), shampoo carpets, and consider painting walls a shade of white or cream. Get rid of any unhealthy-looking plants.

Repair—Make sure all leaky faucets are fixed and shining. Make sure the plumbing, electrical, and cooling and heating systems are in working order. If anything is broken (a step, a railing, a handle), get it fixed.

Fragrance—Rid your house of any unpleasant odors before buyers arrive. Many Realtors like the owners to place potpourri about, or to bake a cake or cinnamon rolls to fill the house with yummy smells.

Neutral colors—Many buyers are turned off by colors they can't move into and work with—if you're repainting or carpeting, stick with variations on beige.

Renovations—If you want to remodel, the two spots that most increase your asking price are the kitchen and bathrooms. Sometimes all you need are new fixtures and fresh curtains.

> **Tip**
>
> If at all possible, sell your current house before you buy another. Trust me; I've neglected to do this twice, and it's a headache to be avoided.

Set the stage—Turn on lights and open draperies before a showing. Homes that "show dark" do not do as well. Softly play some pleasant music in the background. A vase of fresh flowers is a nice touch. Make sure bathroom towels are fresh. Put away valuables. Now run some errands or visit a friend; usually owners leave so Realtors and prospective buyers can talk more freely.

Now let's get you packed and resituated in your new digs. Whether you're moving out of an apartment, condominium, or house, here are fifteen tips to make the process easier:

1. Do the paperwork. Forward your mail to the new address. Transfer insurance, bank accounts, magazine subscriptions, school records, church records, credit cards, medical records and prescriptions, veterinary records, and club memberships. Get a new driver's license if necessary. Order new address labels or stationery. Arrange for phone hookup the day before you move into your new home.

2. Donate or sell unused items. Be merciless—get rid of excess clutter and you'll save on moving costs (which are usually calculated by weight). If you haven't read that book in five years and you never will, or if you're using that exercycle as a valet, let someone else give them a shot.

3. If you're doing a lot of the packing yourself (label these boxes PBO, for Packed By Owner), start gathering cardboard boxes and try to pack a few boxes each day. Begin with items you don't use frequently. This will spread out the work and be much less exhausting.

   Label your linens "Load Last" so you can make up the beds when you arrive. And don't pack extremely valuable items; carry them with you.

   Don't fill any box with items too heavy to lift. Huge boxes are good for lamp shades, but don't fill them with books!

   Use sturdy packing tape—it will open easily when you're ready to unpack, if you just puncture it with a knife or a key.

   Wrap breakables in newspaper or bubble wrap, and cover large slabs of glass or mirrors with an X of masking tape, then pad with packing material (and keep vertical).

   Tip: Blow up and seal Zip-Loc baggies for great packing material for fragile items. Works in the mail, too.

4. Recycle chemicals properly—don't leave paint cans and insecticides for the new owners to dispose of, and don't try to take flammables with you. Drain oil and gas from any lawn equipment.

5. Make sure utilities are turned on in your new home, and that they're turned off in your old one as soon as you're gone.

6. Pack a suitcase for everyone, and include everything you'd need if you were on a weekend vacation. Don't forget an alarm clock, and some snacks to enjoy until you have a working kitchen. Take along some pet treats, too.

7. Give away house plants and perishable food.

8. On moving day, if you have children or pets, consider hiring a sitter so they won't be underfoot as heavy dressers and such are being carried through doorways.

9. If using movers, give them your new phone number, and make sure you're on site when they arrive.

10. Load the vacuum and cleaning tote last, so that you can clean your new home before putting anything away.

11. Don't forget to bring your address book, so you can contact old friends once you arrive.

12. The one item to leave behind is a roll of toilet paper, since you just never know when you're going to make one last trip inside before leaving.

13. Pick up the dry cleaning, and tie up any other loose ends around town.

14. Think of the new residents who'll be living in your old place and leave a clean house behind—either plan time to clean it once everything's out or arrange for a cleaning service. I also like to leave behind a list of my favorite places, so they'll immediately enjoy their new community. Phone numbers of good workers are appreciated, and special instruc-

> Tip
>
> Label each box with the name of the room where it goes, to make unloading easier.

tions for any unusual plants in the yard. Also, maps, concert seating charts, mailbox keys, safe combinations, garage door openers, pool sweeps, the name of the mail deliverer, information about garbage day. Leave behind anything that goes with the house.

15. And, of course, you want to fit into your new community as seamlessly as possible. An air force family I know says the yellow pages are the best place to start. Look up all the hobbies and interests you have, and find out where the people you are likely to become friends with are meeting. In the case of my friend, she immediately finds out where the craft and antique shops, clubs, and guilds are. The local parks and recreation department can fill you in on camps and sports. Volunteer organizations, schools, gyms, libraries, concert halls, amusement parks—everything is in there.

   Additionally, I would suggest you check also with the Visitor's Bureau for community calendars, and subscribe to the local paper, which will list local events.

Chapter Seventeen

Celebrations

✳

When it comes to entertaining and throwing parties, the most important—and yet the most difficult—thing to do is to remember the real meaning of the holiday or event being celebrated, rather than getting stressed-out with all the arrangements and the trappings. (Stressed is desserts spelled backward, you know.) I know it's hard not to be anxious—everybody is coming to your house and you want it to be special. Believe me, I've been there. But looking back at all the stress I've felt, it wasn't actually worth it. I became so exhausted getting everything perfect that I couldn't enjoy the people or convey the very atmosphere of warmth I was trying so hard to achieve! Sometimes I didn't even think about the holiday or the event itself at all, just the details of entertaining.

So if your holiday is Thanksgiving, focus on being grateful for your blessings. Making life-size fabric pilgrims isn't the central idea. And if you're having a Fourth of July barbecue, really reflect on what our Founding Fathers did—and don't worry about sculpting a watermelon.

Listen to Your Mother!

Make your guests feel special by creating a welcoming guest-room. You want your guests to feel pampered, so put yourself in their place: What would really say, "I'm so glad you're here"? These are a few extra touches that will make their stay more comfortable:

Fresh sheets and towels

A teddy bear nestled in the covers

An extra quilt or blanket, folded on a shelf or rack, for easy access

A luggage rack—or an uncluttered table—where they can put their suit-case

An opaque window shade to pull down behind the curtains, if they like dark mornings

A radio alarm clock on the night-stand

Stationery and stamps on a small writing desk, if there's room

A vase of fresh flowers

Some good books and magazines to read

A little goodnight card to rest on their pillow—with some beautifully wrapped chocolates or homemade cookies

A cozy rug on their side of the bed, if you have cold floors

A fluffy robe and slippers in case they left theirs behind

Plenty of closet space and extra hangers

An iron and ironing board

A restful picture, hanging on the wall (or a photo of you with your guest!)

A bedside reading lamp

A guest book for them to sign and comment in

And be sure to see pages 134–135 about making a welcoming guest bath.

Remember, your guests are coming to see you, not your house. And if people are arriving who only want to check out your place—be they friend or relative—why spend your energy worrying about such unkind people? Parties are occasions for all the invited guests to visit and laugh together, to grow closer. Keep your focus on that goal, and don't let it become a contest about judging the rosettes on your petit fours.

My Top Ten
Holiday Entertaining Tips

1. Lower your expectations. One thing your mother probably never told you is that relatives can botch up holidays worse than an uncooked turkey. If you want to celebrate the birth of Christ, choose a quiet, meaningful time when you aren't vacuuming, scrubbing, and decorating to get ready for houseguests. Maybe your remembrance won't even fall on the 25th—maybe you'll choose to help out in a soup kitchen on the 16th, or donate blankets to a shelter on December 4th. Make another day your religious observance so you won't feel cheated out of a meaningful holiday by the hubbub of a party and houseguests. What matters is how you feel in your heart. Then, don't expect Christmas with crazy Uncle Zeppo to be a peaceful, dreamy occasion where you're all gathered around the fire, sipping cocoa. Make your guests comfortable, look for the humor (it's there in every family), and love these guys as best you can.

2. Enlist help. Don't think you have to do it all. Ask everybody to bring something, put people to work setting up chairs, and have a "job list" for people who'd really like to help but don't know what you need done.

3. Corral the kids. Nothing is more boring to children than being dressed up, dragged to a grown-up party, and pinched and told how much bigger they've gotten. Have a separate area where kids can kick off their shoes, play games, make crafts, or watch a movie. Put a little thought into this before they arrive, so you'll be all set. Steer them toward a "Kids Only" table filled with snacks they'll love, so they don't ravage your fruit topiary.

4. Put the emphasis on family closeness. With everything you plan, from meals to games to decorations, think, "Will this bring our family closer together?" Maybe enlarge a picture of great-grandparents to display on an easel. Or make a phone/birthday list of all the far-flung relatives. Plan guessing games that teach you new things about one another. Display scrapbooks on the coffeetable. Tell the family stories behind the recipes you chose for the meal. Talk about what it means to be a member of your extended family or clan. Videotape or record the older generation reminiscing. Post a family tree and encourage everyone to fill in the blanks. Have family T-shirts.

5. Here's another one your mother probably never told you: some holidays are stupid. In other words, you don't *have* to turn your house into a spook alley just because it's Halloween. You don't have to play tricks on April Fool's Day. You don't have to pretend you're Irish every March 17. You don't have to stay up until midnight on New Year's Eve just to watch a ball fall on TV. You can choose the holidays you want to commemorate and how—if you've never really liked turkey at Thanksgiving in the first place, serve prime rib.

You can also go the other way, as I tend to do, and drag out next month's holiday decorations the minute you put last month's away. So what if I like to go overboard on all the holidays, including Mozart's birthday? So what if I put a little Santa hat on the ceramic rooster in my kitchen? I'm an adult, and I enjoy it.

6. Be flexible. Just like travel plans, holiday plans are subject to change, and you need to "roll with the punches" sometimes. Hors d'oeuvre trays get knocked over, people arrive late, the camera runs out of film, a nephew throws up. You can't let mishaps destroy the whole event for you—just know they're coming, and don't get all excited when they do. Better yet, work them into a yearly tradition (well, maybe not the throwing up). I know one family that always has "The Ceremonial Burning of the Christmas Rolls."

We always paint our windows at Christmas, and I like to paint a little mouse asleep in a wreath, his tiny stocking hung on one of the holly sprigs. Well, one year the mouse came out a little large, and my four kids insisted it was a rat. They whooped and laughed, and every year since, they've insisted upon "The Christmas Rat" in the wreath. Now if he comes out too small, I have to wash him off the window and start over.

Bottom line: Big things and little things can disrupt your well-laid plans, but either way, don't get wigged out over your plans. If somebody brought a different salad dressing than the one you planned to use, let it go. If a snowstorm keeps half your family from making the drive, be glad everyone's okay and celebrate the best way you can.

7. If you're having friends over who don't know each other, be a good host or hostess and introduce them. Be sure to mention something they have in common, to break the ice.

8. Do as much as you can ahead of time. Set the table the night before. Plan a menu with mostly items you can make the day before and freeze or chill. You'll save last-minute scrambling, and you may even have time for a relaxing bubble bath before everyone arrives.

9. Mom might not have mentioned this tip, but take anything you don't want seen out of your medicine cabinet. Oh, I know, none of your friends would snoop or gossip about your warts, dandruff, yeast infection, or whatever. Yeah, right. For some reason, folks you would least expect to do it ask to use the bathroom and then somehow open the medicine cabinet. I heard of one woman who stacked marbles in hers so that when someone opened the door they all came clattering out. She lost the friend *and* her marbles!

10. If you're invited to someone else's place, offer to bring something. Even if you are refused, at least bring a house gift—flowers, a crock of jam, and so on. Rave about how wonderful everything looks and tastes, and try not to be someone else's Uncle Zeppo.

Terrific Traditions

If you're keeping up reasonably well with the cleaning, everything else is extra, or as my Louisiana-born husband would say, "lagniappe." Now some of the fun in entertaining is doing extras here and there to make it unusual and memorable. But do these things *only* if you have time and they add to (rather than subtract from) your enjoyment of the holiday. Below I suggest dozens of ideas and traditions to make holidays more fun, but if you did them all, you would be run ragged. Pick and choose the ideas and traditions you really love—things you can enjoy year after year—and don't feel pressured to work yourself into a lather. For even more great holiday ideas, see my book *Family Funbook—More than 400*

Amazing, Amusing, and All-Around Awesome Activities for the Entire Family! (Running Press, 1998).

New Year's

✳ Deliver a New Year's package to a neighbor—include noise-makers, a sparkling drink, toasting goblets, confetti, and hats.

✳ Fix black-eyed peas for good luck, a Southern tradition.

✳ Hang a calendar featuring seasonal family photos.

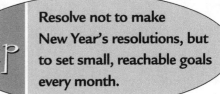

Resolve not to make New Year's resolutions, but to set small, reachable goals every month.

✳ Write a New Year's love letter to your kids, praising their accomplishments of the past year.

✳ To keep the house from looking so bare when you put the Christmas decorations away, leave out a display of snowmen.

✳ Put gold and silver poppers on your guests' pillows.

Valentine's Day

✳ Scout tag sales and antique shops for red plates—they don't have to match—and set a whole table in red dishes.

✳ Tie goblets or candlesticks with a pink bow.

✳ Make two teardrop shapes, using clumps of birch twigs. Tie the "points" together and you have a rustic heart wreath. Tie with a raffia bow.

✳ Make heart-shaped food: pancakes, pizza, cookies, cakes.

✳ Use colored chalk to draw red hearts leading up the walkway to your door.

✳ Give a neighbor a "heart attack." While they're gone, stick hearts (glued to wire or twigs), or flowers, all up and down their walkway to welcome them home.

✳ Dot a white lamp shade with pink and red hearts.

✳ Stick conversation hearts on a chunky white or purple candle—use melted paraffin for "glue."

St. Patrick's Day

✳ Fix a traditional corned beef dinner, or make an entire meal where everything's green, even dessert. Some ideas: limeade, green salad, split pea soup, green pasta, green beans, pesto sauce, spinach souffle, curried rice, broccoli, green olives, pickles, grapes, pistachio cake, key lime pie, spumoni ice cream, mints.

✳ Make dinner rolls that look like shamrocks—just use frozen bread dough rolled into three small balls per muffin tin.

✳ Buy some Irish music and wake up the family to a festive St. Patrick's Day.

✳ For kids, hide gold-covered chocolate coins throughout the house, and see if they can find all the "gold coins" left by the leprechauns. For a variation, cover real coins with a hint of glitter.

Easter

✳ Grow real grass in an Easter basket. Three weeks ahead of time, fill a plastic plant saucer with dirt and grass seeds, and keep moist.

✶ Arrange an egg hunt for visitors, kids, *or* adults. For adults, simply fill the eggs with more sophisticated candies and gifts.

✶ Thaw frozen bread dough, roll it into three long "snakes," and braid. Bring ends together to form a bird's nest, and place on a greased baking sheet. Now tuck five raw, colored eggs in between the pieces of dough. Sprinkle with multi-color candy sprinkles. Bake as you would a loaf of bread, and the eggs will cook as well. This is reminiscent of a grand Easter tradition in Italy.

✶ Make a religious centerpiece using items that depict the real meaning of Easter. Kids will enjoy guessing what each item refers to—a rock for the stone that was rolled away, a nail for the nails that were driven into Jesus' hands, a piece of wood for the cross, muslin for the cloth his body was wrapped in, and so on.

✶ Place a vase of tulips or daffodils on the nightstand in your guest room.

✶ Place a stuffed rabbit upside down in a silk plant—only let his bottom and feet show—it will look like he's trying to hide.

April Fool's Day

✶ Throw an April Fool's party—invite everyone to bring their best story about a practical joke or prank.

✶ Serve food that's decorated to look like something else:

Meat loaf can be "frosted" with mashed potatoes to look like a cake.

Tuna, crab, and chicken salads can be molded into various shapes.

Funny faces and people can be "sculpted" by arranging fruits and veggies with toothpicks: cabbage heads, carrot noses, red pepper lips, and so on.

Marzipan candies often look like carrots and other vegetables.

Frosting can be piped over a flat slice of cake to look like pasta. Drizzle with strawberry syrup to look like marinara sauce.

* Don't forget to have a Spam-carving contest.

* And, when your guests arrive, greet them in a bathrobe and pretend you knew nothing about the party—someone must have played a trick on *you!* Then invite them in for a fun evening.

May Day

* Make cones from paper doilies, fill them with flowers, and attach a ribbon handle. Hang on the doors of friends and neighbors.

* Make May Day cookies. Use chocolate frosting to "glue" half a Reese's Peanut Butter Cup onto a round cookie. This forms the basket. Now pipe on a handle with brown frosting in a tube. Dab more frosting where the flowers would go, and sprinkle on flower-shaped cake decorations.

* Paint a flower pot and plant a bright bloom inside.

* Hot glue silk blossoms to a vest.

Mother's Day

✦ Borrow a lab coat, a wig, and funny glasses. Now arrive at your mother's door with all the supplies necessary, and—with a funny accent—inform her that her daughter has purchased a pedicure for her. Sit your mom down, soak her feet in a bucket of suds, and give her a wonderful foot treatment! (Even more fun if you can arrange for some of her friends to be over, and bring some of yours to help.) This could also be a facial or makeup session.

> **Tip**
> For a pretty centerpiece, cover a cake pedestal with seasonal fruits and flowers, and place a pastel candle in the middle.

✦ Fill a scrapbook with old family photos, but under each one write, "I love you because . . ." and tell why that picture depicts another reason you love your mom.

✦ Sit down with your mom, two coloring books, and some crayons to relive a moment from your childhood, when the two of you sat and colored together. (Or recreate another childhood memory.)

✦ Invite your mother over for dinner, and fix something she showed you how to make.

✦ If you live in a neighborhood or apartment where there are lots of moms whose kids live far away, throw a luncheon for all of them to get together. Bragging about grandkids is a must!

✦ Take your mom to a tea room or a fashion show.

✦ Call a photographer and arrange for a family portrait.

✦ Give Mom some gussied-up toothpicks to use next time she has a party and serves hors d'oeuvres. Hot glue tiny shells, small silk flowers, or buttons to one end of each toothpick, and present them in a drawstring pouch or in a burlap "envelope" with one of the toothpicks serving as a straight pin to hold it closed.

Father's Day

✳ Give Dad a blast from the past—find and give him toys, candies, and games from his childhood. Did he always want a little red wagon? What kind of gum did he chew? Did he like yo-yos, science sets, sports? Can you find a toy replica of his first car? How about an eight-track tape or an LP record?

 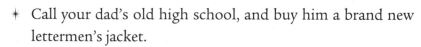 Compile a family cookbook. Don't forget "recipes" from the kids.

✳ Call your dad's old high school, and buy him a brand new lettermen's jacket.

✳ Use a 45-rpm record for the bow on a gift (less than a dollar in thrift shops). Choose an oldie with a song title that hints at the gift inside.

✳ Transfer his most handsome photo to fabric (major copier stores can do this), then fabric-glue it to a pillow.

✳ Make him a special trophy. Think of a meaningful (or comical) achievement of his, and honor him with an engraved plaque or trophy. Is he master of the barbecue grill? Has he gotten too many speeding tickets? Does he win an award for paying for the most weddings? Is he king of the remote control?

✳ Find all his old buddies, teachers, and so on and get them on videotape raving (and exaggerating) about what a talented, wonderful genius he was.

✳ Have a luau—be sure to give him a Hawaiian shirt, a co-
conut, anything in keeping with the theme. How about
surfboard-shaped cookies?

Fourth of July

✳ Make ice cream without an ice cream maker. This works for
kids or adults, and everyone's amazed at the yummy results. I
did this with weekend visitors at a fireworks show, and they
were as dazzled by the ice cream as by the fireworks! Here's
how you do it: Pour 1 cup whipping cream, 1 tablespoon
sugar, and 1 teaspoon vanilla (or other flavored extract) into a
small Zip-Loc bag. Seal it shut. Now place it inside a larger Zip-
Loc bag, along with 12 ice cubes and 2 tablespoons salt. Seal
the larger bag closed, and turn the whole package over and
over for about ten to fifteen minutes, or until ice cream begins
to form in the smaller bag. It gets cold—you might want to
wear gloves! When ready to sample your creation, remove the
smaller sealed bag and pour its contents into a cup or bowl.

✳ Arrange a display of teddy bears wearing red-white-and-
blue bows. One or two could display a small American flag
or wear a tiny triangle hat made of newspaper.

✳ Sew or glue red and white ribbon to a rectangular pillow,
like the stripes of a flag. Attach a square of star-printed
navy fabric to the upper left-hand corner, or use a square of
solid navy and sew on white buttons for the stars.

✳ Display an American flag. Attach the bracket to your home
and proudly wave the red, white, and blue.

✳ String a garland of red, white, and blue paper stars. Hang
from a mantel, window, or doorway.

✴ Make a bouquet of American flags, and display in a vase as you would flowers.

✴ Make and frame a roughly needlepointed swatch of muslin that says, "Give Me Liberty or Give Me Death."

✴ Paint a white beach umbrella with red and blue stars.

Halloween

✴ Scatter oversized paper autumn leaves down the dining table.

✴ Make autumn candlesticks, using autumn fruits and tiny pumpkins on a skewer.

✴ Serve cinnamon cider in a "boiling cauldron" to trick-or-treaters. Really, it's just seasoned cider poured into a black witch's pot—dry ice forms the "smoke."

✴ Now that the weather has turned colder, make sure you have plenty of room in your entry closet for visitors' coats and wraps.

✴ Sponge-paint black cats and paw prints on an orange shirt.

✴ Cut eerie silhouettes in paper lunch sacks, then place sand and a votive candle in the bottom of each. Line them up along your walkway as luminarias.

✴ Joni's Favorites ✴

Make a "Witch Crash." We nail this to a tree in our front yard every Halloween, and it's a hit with neighbors and passers-by (some even photograph it). You make it look as though a witch was flying low and splatted right into a tree (or a post or wall). Stick wood into the arms of a black sweatshirt, and tape green rubber gloves onto the cuffs. Nail the arms onto either side of the tree, then stick wood into the legs of black pants, and use black tape to fasten on ugly black boots. Nail the pants bottom and legs under the sweatshirt, legs straddling the tree. Nail on a black garbage bag for a cape. Nail a long, frizzy wig above the sweatshirt, and a pointy black witch's hat over the wig (it will look as if her face is embedded in the tree). Hilarious!

Thanksgiving

✳ Baste the turkey with melted butter.

✳ Pour melted butter over the vegetables.

✳ Whip melted butter and softened cream cheese into the mashed potatoes.

✳ Sprinkle butter and brown sugar over the squash or yams.

✳ Dot fruit pies with butter before putting on the top crust.

✳ Slather butter on the homemade rolls.

✳ Tomorrow, make an appointment for a cholesterol test.

But seriously . . .

✳ Make a whimsical turkey by placing a pine cone on its side, and gluing autumn leaves to the wide end, fanned out to form a tail.

✳ Help kids learn gratitude by helping them write a thank you note to someone who serves them—a bus driver, a postal worker, the grocery clerk.

✳ Hang a grouping of Indian corn on your door, tied with a raffia bow.

✳ Display pumpkins in odd number: turn one on its side to show the stem, for visual interest.

✳ Start a Journal of Appreciation. Look for the good in your life and jot it down in a notebook.

✳ Give a jar of popcorn kernels to a neighbor, with your thanks.

Hanukkah

✦ Make a cupcake menorah—instead of candles, place white-frosted cupcakes on each point of a menorah, then light a candle in each of the cupcakes.

✦ Make a Star of David tablecloth—using a round white cloth, measure and mark two overlapping triangles. With fabric glue, attach flat blue braiding over the marks.

✦ Make blue bath crystals, pour them into a pretty jar, and tie with a silver ribbon. Here's the easy recipe: In a large bowl, stir together 1 cup of epsom salts, 1 teaspoon of glycerine (available in pharmacies), 12 drops food coloring, and 25 drops of scented oil. Mix thoroughly.

✦ Make eight teacup candles. Scout out second-hand shops and garage sales for pretty blue and white cups and saucers, then purchase wicks from a craft store. Fill with melted paraffin, then line them up menorah-style, down the center of your table.

Christmas

✦ Make black-and-white photocopies of family pictures—use this paper to wrap smaller gifts. Color copies would be a wonderful, albeit expensive, alternative.

✦ Have a holiday cookie exchange. This is a great way to unify an apartment building or neighborhood. Everyone brings a plate of goodies, and you all get to take home samples of the various contributions.

✦ Invite friends or family to a full day of cookie-baking. Each person brings a recipe plus an assigned ingredient, such as flour, sugar, butter, and so on. You each make enough cookies to give to everyone on your Christmas list. (Cute aprons would be a fun gift to give each of your guests.)

✦ Hang a wreath on the grill of your car.

✦ Wear a garland of silk holly in your hair.

✦ Tuck twinkle lights into the greenery on a mantle or banister.

✦ If you live where it doesn't snow, spray paint your bushes white, so it will look like it did.

✦ If your family is "gifted out," get together anyway, and instead of a gift exchange, have everybody contribute to a good cause and deliver the toys, money, blankets, whatever, to the charity you choose.

✦ If you have the space, keep a fully decorated Christmas tree in a closet to save annual decorating and undecorating.

✦ Keep a basket of ornaments by your door and give one to every visitor.

✦ Have a tree-trimming party—you'll be amazed at how fast the tree gets decorated! Then, go caroling.

✦ Joni's Favorites ✦

One of our favorite traditions in the Hilton household is to watch holiday performances, such as *The Nutcracker*.

✦ If you are divorced and sharing custody of your children, you'll probably spend every other Christmas without your kids. Don't despair—have your own Christmas all over again when they return in January (and take advantage of the after-Christmas sales!).

✦ Tie throw pillows to look like presents, with big, fluffy bows.

✴ Stir drinks with cinnamon sticks.

✴ Sprinkle fake snow around a display of snowmen.

✴ Hang Christmas cards on a length of ribbon strung high in a doorway.

✴ Nestle votive candles in rock salt for a glowing, snowy centerpiece.

✴ Spray frost on the corners of your windows.

✴ Buy a fluffy white greenhouse-grown chrysanthe-mum at the supermarket, and tuck in ac-cents of red and green—such as artificial picks of cranberries and pine from a local craft shop.

Simmer water with a pinch of cinnamon, cloves, and orange rind to fill the house with wonderful smells.

✴ Play Christmas music.

✴ Make pancakes using eggnog instead of milk (you may never go back).

✴ Display a photo of the family pet wearing fake reindeer antlers.

Kwanzaa

✴ See the Hanukkah idea using teacups, but use seven teacups—red, green, or black—letting each one represent one of the Kwanzaa virtues.

✴ Paint your own Kikombe cha umoja, or Unity Cup, using the latest paints for glass, available in craft shops.

✴ Sew a Kwanzaa scarf. Use a blanket stitch (or any stitch you like) to attach eight twelve-inch squares of fleece in the traditional colors of Black Unity—red, green, gold, and black—together in a long strip.

✳ Make Kwanzaa stationery. In pretty cursive, write the seven Kwanzaa principles around the edge of a sheet of paper:

Unity—Umoja
Self-determination—Kujichagulia
Collective work and responsibility—Ujima
Cooperative economics—Ujamma
Purpose—Nia
Creativity—Kuumba
Faith—Imani

Now photocopy your sheet using colored ink, or copy onto colored paper, and you have a stack of stationery to give your house guests.

Chapter Eighteen

Decorating Secrets

The easiest way to decorate is to surround yourself with things you love—colors, shapes, patterns, objects. Your home has to say "you" before you'll really be happy there. If you try to copy someone else's style, or the cover of a magazine, you'll never feel your place is really yours.

Many of us hesitate to use our familiar "stuff," convinced that we have to hide our everyday things in the closet or trade them in for the latest trends and styles. But as long as you know the basics of good decorating, you can incorporate your own spin into any look you want.

The Basic Rules of Decorating

1. First, think classic. It's the same with clothes—you'll get more life out of a tailored jacket than hot pink capris. I'm not saying your whole home has to be cautious and careful, but you might want to stick with traditional pieces when it comes to the expensive stuff, such as a sofa or a hutch that would dominate a room. Then, just as you can jazz up that basic jacket with a scarf or pin, you can jazz up your sofa with paintings, throw pillows, and interesting end tables.

2. Next, especially if your home is small, think double-duty. Whenever possible, make each piece earn its place in your home—a sofa must also fold out into a guest bed, a table must double as office space, a bench must conceal storage under the seat. Getting more than one use from some items saves having to buy additional pieces.

3. Think spare. Realtors always advise home sellers to "uncrowd" their rooms so that the home will seem larger and sell better. Why not live this way all the time? Get rid of little-used extra tables, stools, racks, and knickknacks that increase your clutter quotient (and your cleaning time).

4. Be brave. Show your adventurous side *somewhere*. Maybe it will be a trellis on the ceiling—laden with silk wisteria—in a guest bath where you can close the door. Or maybe you'll lean a wild art piece on the mantel or above a breakfast table. But do express your personality in your home. It will seem more artfully decorated if there are some surprises, some daring colors here and there. A red throw pillow, a yellow plant pot, a speckled rooster, an oversized flag, a street sign, a blue basket—accents don't need to be beige or taupe.

5. Create space. You can create the illusion of larger rooms several ways: Unclutter all that you can—and donate things to a good charity. Mirror a wall or hang a large mirror to carry the eye further. Install plenty of bright lighting. Choose pastel shades of paint and fabric. Buy smaller pieces of furniture so the room isn't overwhelmed with overstuffed couches or enormous sideboards. Paint the ceiling white. Then again, another school of thought is to enjoy a small room's coziness and use the colors and items you enjoy, even if they "bring the walls in."

6. Scour flea markets and second-hand shops for intriguing chairs, cabinets, and other pieces that you could paint or decoupage. You'll save a bundle, get a one-of-a-kind conversation piece, and enjoy investing your time and talent in redoing your own furniture.

7. To create warmth and a sense of welcome, use cuddly throws, plenty of pillows, and area rugs. A slipcover can brighten an old sofa, and fresh flowers add joy to any room.

Knockout Decorating Ideas

✶ Don't have a fireplace to "anchor" your living room? Make one! A mantel over two posts can provide the architectural detail, then the "fireplace" can be covered with a mirror, a screen, staggered heights of thick candles, or a flower arrangement.

✶ Run a thick, gold ribbon down the center of your dining table. Place candles along it or a pretty plant in the middle for a centerpiece.

✶ Add life to your lamp shades—stick photos, flowers, buttons, or fabric trim to them.

✶ Use a framed mirror as a tray on your dining table, to hold candles and reflect their light.

✶ Attach legs to a pretty tray to make a small table.

Tip

Keep newspaper clippings from turning yellow by soaking them for an hour in a solution of 1 quart club soda and 1 milk of magnesia tablet.

✳ Hide conspicuous work areas with standing screens. If you have a messy desk or office area in your living room (which is sometimes a necessary arrangement), conceal it. Screens can be wood, framed fabric, wrought iron, wallpapered, hand-painted—shop for the right size, then add the finish you like best.

✳ Frame a collection of flat items—dried flowers, love notes, doilies, ancestral photos, baby clothes, old valentines, cartoons.

✳ If you need a kitchen island, consider a chopping block, a farmhouse table, even a wide bookcase (think of the storage!).

✳ Joni's Favorites ✳

For a crisp, clean look in any room, try painting the walls a bold primary color, then trim all molding and woodwork with glossy white.

✳ Let a wicker tea cart hold towels in a spacious bathroom—or quilts in a bedroom.

✳ Establish a file of decorating ideas; clip magazine pictures for future reference. Save all paint chips, names of stores where you purchased items, and receipts.

✳ Enliven "blah" cabinet doors with decorative knobs. Sometimes this is all a kitchen needs.

✳ Use black to accent warm wood tones.

✳ If you just can't think how to change the look of a room, take everything out and start over. Have two huge trash bags handy—one for things to throw away, and one for things "I'll deal with later." You'll be amazed at how much stuff you decide not to put back.

✳ Turn containers on their side and hang them on the wall for shelves—square baskets, tin boxes, wooden crates, a tiny trunk. All can add interest as well as function.

* Hang your towels from something you picked up in your travels or at a flea market.

* Keep garlic or onions in a wire birdcage.

* Hang a row of old-fashioned hats on one wall.

* If you have three small prints you want to hang, consider hanging them vertically, one above the other.

* Drape your bed with mosquito netting and place potted palms nearby to create an exotic retreat. Cover a chair seat with an animal print fabric.

* If using both paint and wallpaper in one room, match the paint to the background color of the wallpaper.

* Hang a small wooden chair on the wall, Shaker style.

* Make planters out of unusual objects—a teacup for tiny plants, a cookie jar or biscuit tin, a teapot.

> **Tip**
>
> Keep a donation box or bag in a closet. Every month, schedule a donation drop-off at your favorite charity or thrift shop. It will force you to constantly get rid of things you no longer need.

* Have a favorite phrase? Stencil or paint it on a wall somewhere in your home. I made up a phrase one Thanksgiving, and later asked an artist friend to paint it under the mantel in our dining room. It says, "How blessed we are to have friends we would choose as relatives, and relatives we would choose as friends."

* No time to dust for company? Turn out all the lights and light a bunch of candles instead.

* Arrange a framed theme: A picture of your grandpa who loved to garden next to his old gardening gloves framed

behind glass. Antique seed packets or garden tools could also be added. A photo of mom in the kitchen, plus a framed apron and some utensils, would be great in the kitchen—and how about a framed favorite recipe?

✴ Drape a tablecloth over a curtain rod for instant lace curtains. Here are some other great window treatment ideas: a row of bandannas, folded point-down and hung from the top of the window; gauzy netting tied into luscious poofs; stenciling around a window instead of hanging fabric; looping fabric over a painted wooden rod; and using sheer fabric gathered on two tension rods to create privacy yet allow light through.

✴ Hang shutters on either side of a garden-view window.

✴ If you break a piece of china, save the pieces. Cover a flowerpot with wet plaster, and press the broken pieces into the plaster. You can also make tabletops and picture or mirror frames this way.

✴ Frame a collection of kitschy junk from your childhood, the trendier the better. Mount it on a background of fabric from the era. Friends will see your display and say, "Oh, I remember those bracelets! And you still have one of those hair things? Cool!"

✴ If you find a fabric you love, but can't afford to cover a chair or sofa with it, buy half a yard and make a throw pillow.

✴ Buy a bunch of small, inexpensive frames—all the same metal finish—and fill them with favorite photos to display on a table.

✴ Hang a map and pin ribbons to mark everywhere you travel.

✳ Shop second-hand stores for picture frames—ignore the velvet Elvis it surrounds; just use the frame (and maybe spray paint it gold?).

✳ Paint the interior back side of a bookcase a bold color, since most of it won't show. (How about wallpapering that same surface?)

✳ What's your ancestry? Honor it with a collection of items from that country, hung on the wall or displayed on a table.

> **Tip**
> When filling a bookcase, break up the "weighty" feel of the books with an occasional art object or framed photo.

Keeping Plants in Your Home

Houseplants contribute much to the enjoyment of your home. They're not quite companions in the sense that pets are, but they still depend on you for their sustenance, and they respond with beauty, blossoms, and freshness that add a vitality and sense of life and nature to your environment. They also purify the air we breathe and add a beautiful decorating accent. And also, it just plain feels good to grow things.

My dad was a master gardener, among other talents, and we used to tease him that he could find a cigarette butt on the ground, take it home, and make it grow. Some people do seem to have the gift. But whether you do or not, you can enjoy—and decorate with—greenery by following these easy steps.

How Many?

Depending on how serious a gardener you are, and how green your thumb is, you'll need to decide how many plants are right for you. Many apartment dwellers and new homeowners discover the joy of growing their own herbs and veggies in window pots, or creating a lush corner of ferns and exotic blossoms. But be honest: Will you spend a portion of your week feeding, watering, dusting, and removing the dead foliage from a dozen or more indoor plants? If not, or if you travel a lot and need people to water your plants, you should opt for fewer plants than someone who has time to tend a large collection. Start with two or three and see how they do.

You can have more plants if you choose ones that are fairly easy to grow and that withstand more neglect than the average plant. Here are some excellent low-maintenance plants to consider:

Ivy—This is super hardy; you almost can't kill it. Best of all, you can train it into a topiary shape with some wire and pruning shears.

Dieffenbachia—This has broad, speckled leaves and thrives with little attention. It's a great choice for bathrooms, as it enjoys humidity. Its common name is Dumbcane.

Pothos—This is an extremely easy to grow vine with variegated, heart-shaped leaves.

Aspidistra—Called the "Cast Iron" plant, it survives neglect beautifully. It has dark green, broad-blade leaves.

Corn plants—These resemble actual corn stalks; they're very hardy, but will grow quite tall—I have one touching a fifteen-foot ceiling in my family room.

Dracaena—Look for the variety with long, curving leaves edged with pink and yellow. They're similar in appearance to corn plants.

Fatsia—These bushes need a good amount of space to spread. They have lobed or hand-shaped leaves, and can grow about five feet tall.

Spider Plant—These do best hanging, and send out little fireworks-shaped starts, which you can cut to create new plants. Some folks call them airplane plants. They do best with plenty of humidity.

Bromeliads and Cacti—Check out various varieties; they're colorful and easy to grow as well.

Caladium—These are great for color variety, as the leaves are often pink with red veins and green edges.

Tip **Marigolds repel pests.**

Asparagus fern—I like these for variety of texture in a grouping of plants. They're spiky and light green, and look good cascading down the side of a pot.

Spathiphyllum—Except that my cats love to eat it, this is a gorgeous plant also known as the Peace Lily. It has broad, deep green leaves and delicate white blooms.

Aloe—Thick and spiny-edged, this succulent has stems that can be cut and used medicinally for bites and burns.

Ficus and rubber plants—Both can grow into fairly large trees, but they're also a cinch to grow.

If you find you react adversely to molds and spores, which thrive in damp soil, you may have to reduce—or eliminate—the number of plants you keep. An excess number of plants can also increase the humidity in your home.

Watering

Whichever kind of plant you choose, make sure you give it the optimum environment so it can thrive: the right amount of

Listen to Your Mother!

It's good to know which house plants can be toxic if eaten by kids or animals. Be extra cautious if you have any of these:

Philodendrons, pathos, and ivies—All parts are poisonous, including the berry when it flowers.

Dieffenbachia—All parts are poisonous, especially the stems.

Jerusalem cherry—This produces fruits that resemble peppers, but don't eat them.

Holly, yews, mistletoe, poinsettias—What a shame that these lovely holiday plants are dangerous if eaten. Be especially sure not to have white berries of the mistletoe where anyone could mistakenly swallow them.

If you suspect that anyone has ingested any of these plants, call your city's Poison Control Center. Many outdoor plants are also toxic; teach kids not to nibble on anything you didn't approve of. Even if the plant itself is safe, you never know what poisons, pesticides, or contaminants could be on it.

sunlight and the right amount of water. Most plants come with tags that explain ideal conditions. If yours didn't, call an expert at the nursery and find out where your plant will be happiest. Get all the care and feeding information you can.

One of the biggest mistakes new plant owners make is over-watering. You'll know if your plant is getting too much water if the lower leaves turn pale yellow, and the stems get soft and mushy. If the soil feels damp an inch below the surface, it's wet enough and doesn't need any more watering yet. Some plants prefer constant moisture; others do better if you let them dry out a bit. Again, consult an expert to find out which kind your plant is.

Tip
Plant dill by tomato plants to prevent tomato worms.

When it is time to water, don't use ice-cold water; room temperature is best (and for this reason, do not use an ice cube to time-delay watering; it will still be too cold as it melts). Occasionally stir a spoonful of plant food, into your watering can (about every two to three months). Mist the leaves with a spray bottle every day or so, or use a vaporizer to replace moisture in a heated winter home.

It's also important not to let a plant sit in acrid water, but to let it drain and rinse fresh water through. If you get a plant wrapped in florist's paper, remove the paper and place the pot in another container. Then, when you water it, the water will drain through to the outside pot where you can empty it and keep the plant well-drained.

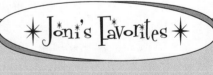

✳ Joni's Favorites ✳

I recommend giving plants a little plant food every few months, and I like the Miracle-Gro brand.

Another way to insure that the roots are not sitting in water is to place pebbles, stones, or charcoal in the bottom of the pot, below the dirt where the plant is growing. Water can then drain through the dirt to this rocky layer, then out the bottom. Remember, there needs to be oxygen in that soil, as well as water, and good drainage will ensure that your plant's roots are not mired in a soggy puddle.

Light and Heat

All plants need light, though house plants generally like filtered or reflected light. Think before you place a plant in a bright window; the direct sunlight and heat may be too strong there. Also, the plant might dry out more quickly. And take note if your plant is sitting near a heating or air-conditioning vent; both can dry it out. If the leaves are curling or turning crisp, your plant needs more humidity (move it to the bathroom and let it enjoy the vapor when you shower).

Just as it's possible to waterlog a plant, it's possible to dry it out. The easiest way this happens is by using unconditioned clay pots, which draw moisture away from the soil. To prevent this, immerse new clay pots in water until all hissing and air bubbles cease. Glazed or plastic pots shouldn't have as much problem.

If your light source is directional, you'll want to turn your plants occasionally, so they'll grow straight instead of leaning in one direction.

Pruning and Pinching

If you have a branching plant that tends to get "leggy," you can pinch off the top stems to make the plant fill in nearer the base and look bushier. This "pinching" is just pulling off the unwanted areas with your fingers, or snipping them with plant clippers. I once knew of a woman who thought pinching

meant she should squeeze all the leaves on
the plant—which obviously did not
help her situation.

You can shape plants quite simply
by removing any area where you don't
want the plant sending nourishment—if you
want a tree to get taller, clip off any limbs sprouting by the
ground. If you want a bush to widen instead of getting so tall,
cut off the top.

Protecting Floors and Furniture

Water needs to drain out of pots, but the last thing you want is
a permanent ring on carpet, floors, or furniture underneath
the plant. Elevate your container to keep it from making direct
contact with these surfaces by using a plant stand, casters, a
rack, a hook for hanging, or small pads sold just for this purpose. Even bunion pads will work.

Cut Flowers

Bouquets add beauty and fragrance to any room and lift our
spirits unlike anything else. To help yours last as long as possible, try these tips:

✳ Refrigerate the flowers when you're away from home, or
while you're asleep.

✳ Remove any leaves below the water level so they won't decay
and spoil the water.

✳ Keep ends freshly cut on an angle, so they can absorb more
water. If stems are especially thick, split them. Many florists

recommend cutting stems under water to avoid any air contact with the fresh cut.

✴ Add lemon-lime soda to the water. A spoonful of sugar, an aspirin, or a few drops of chlorine bleach are also ways to keep blooms fresh longer.

Make tulips stand up straight in the vase by dropping a penny into the water.

✴ To keep cut flowers in place, use a florist's "frog," a ball of wire mesh, or a gridwork of invisible tape placed over the mouth of the container.

Artificial Flowers

You can enjoy the beauty of blooming flowers all year if you choose a realistic-looking artificial arrangement. Even artificial trees and foliage can dress up a dark corner where nothing "real" might be able to grow, and they certainly don't require as much care! However, they do collect dust and need hosing off outside, or rinsing off in the shower from time to time.

I have a friend whose windowless laundry room is made brighter and more welcoming by a row of potted geraniums—and there's not a real one in the bunch. With silk plants, just make sure you buy top quality, so they really do look real.

Chapter Nineteen

Enjoying Your Home

You've cleaned, you've scrubbed, you've made repairs—you have mad skills, Honey. You also now have a safe, healthy home you can be proud of. But to truly enjoy living in it, you need a few more tricks. You need to doll up the place, as my grandmother might say.

Sound

Stand in your living room and listen. Hear anything? What—no music? Shop carefully for a music system—is your place large enough to accommodate those huge theater speakers men seem unable to live without? Today there are so many great sound systems on the market, and most units not only sound good but look good. However, after shopping, you might decide all you need is a simple radio/CD player. The point is to be able to enjoy beautiful music in your home; you don't have to create a recording studio. And you don't have to play music all the time, just when you want to.

What other sounds do you enjoy? Birds? Wind chimes? Water tumbling over rocks? Look for CDs of sounds that soothe you.

Are you a television watcher? If so, place your TV where you will most often sit to watch it. Don't let it dominate the room unless it dominates your life. I am not anti-TV; I used to host a television talk show in Los Angeles, and my husband is a TV news anchor. But I believe in selective viewing and in choosing shows to watch rather than flipping through the channels simply to kill time. Living beautifully takes creativity and involvement; television watching is passive.

> **Tip:** Elevate the back row in your video cabinet, so you can see all the movies you have.

Scent

Now breathe deeply. Smell anything? The scent of a clean house is exactly that: clean. There are no traces of bacteria in the air. But some folks like to add fragrance, and if you do, there are many ways to do it. Several have already been mentioned, such as scented oil on light bulbs and air-conditioning filters, and bowls of potpourri. Here are some other ideas.

✳ Room sprays. These can be delicate, or surprisingly heavy; you need to experiment with what you like.

✳ Solid wicks. These are good for masking unpleasant odors, but they are not the most attractive; hide them behind something and replace when they "evaporate."

✳ Candles. Some emit their perfume even without being lit (as with scented wax chips). They're pretty and they do the job; just don't light one and forget about it.

✳ Simmering beads. These typically have delicious food aromas, such as apple-cinnamon, vanilla, strawberry, blueberry, and such. Again, as with candles, you want to keep an eye on anything simmering on the stove. Don't let all the water simmer out; the beads and pan will start burning. You can make your own simmering mixture by dropping a bit of cinnamon, cloves, and orange peel into a pot of heated water.

✳ Plug-in air fresheners. These are great for small areas, but they are visible, and they don't last long. Replace frequently.

✳ Fresh flowers. Nothing smells like the real thing. If you can afford it, load up. (See also "Cut Flowers" in chapter 18.)

✳ Packaged sachets. I prefer these in drawers and closets, but they can actually add scent to an entire room; they're a nice touch resting on the pillows of a guest bed.

> ✳ Joni's Favorites ✳
>
> **I love toilet paper roll fillers—tubes of little scented beads that emit fragrance whenever the roll is pulled— for scenting a bathroom.**

Sight

What does your place do for you, visually? Most people paint their walls a neutral shade, buy a neutral sofa, and stick with neutral carpeting. And there is nothing wrong with this safe route to decorating; you can always add color with throw pillows and paintings. But it's more fun to try some other ways to jazz up the decor. Chapter 18 contains a wealth of decorating ideas, and here are a few more ways to add interest for the eye:

Make sure to have your sofa facing the fireplace (or a mantel used to anchor the room), or use two love seats, facing each other, perpendicular to the fireplace, and separated by a small coffee table (love seats allow you more flexibility in room arranging).

Speaking of coffee tables, you might want one that provides storage space. A passenger trunk works well, as does a wicker trunk, a wooden chest, or a barrel cut in half and topped with thick glass. I've even seen tabletops placed over a stack of colorful luggage or over antique birdcages. Browse through second-hand shops and garage sales for cast-off treasures; think how you could paint or refinish an old table. Open up your options by looking at standard-size tables and having the legs cut shorter.

As always, scour "bone yards" for architectural pieces such as iron gates, mantels, pillars, ceiling tins, corbels—how might they work into your decorating scheme?

The space above doorways can be fun places to display things—put up a shelf or hang the items right on the wall. These could be a row of hats, a plate rack, a wreath, a shelf of teapots, a plaque, a horizontal painting, a stencil, or even something I did in my daughter's room—hang picket fence flower boxes and fill them with silk flowers and stuffed bunnies.

Make lamps out of found containers—just about anything hollow can be threaded with lighting cords and made into a lamp base. Lighting supply stores can show you how simply this can be done. If you have a hanging lamp, consider wrapping the chain with a fabric sleeve that matches your furniture, scrunching it up so there's plenty on the chain.

If you have a banister or railing, wrap it with silk greenery, and change the look each season, using flower picks. Or wrap with sheer fabric for a filmy, feminine look.

Color and Your Personality

You've probably been told you're a certain season of the year, and you should wear certain colors to bring out your best skin tones.

Most colorists will hold scarves of varying fabrics up to your face, and you'll see how certain tones bring out your eyes or cheek color, while others make you look ashen or pallid. They usually assign you a season, and it follows these rules:

Winter people: Usually they have dark or silver hair, light skin, and look best in navy, black, pure white, deep purple, true red, fuschia, forest green, dark gray, any intense cool color.

Spring people: Usually they have yellow undertones in their skin. Blondes will be golden or reddish, brunettes will be auburn. They look best in yellow-toned pinks, oranges, yellow-greens, turquoise, peach, salmon, medium yellows, lilac purples, and most blues.

Summer people: Usually summers have pink undertones in their skin and pale blue eyes. Blondes will be silvery-white blonde, as opposed to golden. They look best in all kinds of pastels, especially pinks and blues. Cool, light colors flatter most.

Autumn people: These are the darker-skinned, brown-haired folks with Irish-setter brown eyes. They look best in rust, olive green, cranberry, gold, cream, brown, burnt orange, deep (but not navy) blue. Pinks should be almost coral-red, and purples more plum than lilac.

There's something to this; we all know what colors we're wearing when we get the most compliments. But we need not be so rigid as to confine ourselves to one season and one season only (what if there were five seasons?).

When decorating your home, use the colors that make your heart sing. If you're technically a spring-colored person who should wear peach and salmon, but you love dark green and brick red country decorating, forget the springtime dictate and bring in the cows.

My sister-in-law's home is modern and dramatic—black, silver, gold, shrimp, cream—and she's a summer. But her house looks dynamite, and she looks dynamite in it.

Certain colors do affect our moods, and within every color, you can probably find a shade you like—and even one that matches your skin tone, if you must. Here are the "personalities" of various colors:

White—Crisp and clean, white symbolizes purity. But it's also a great accent for dark colors—it sharpens lines and freshens a room. Truly white paint is easy to match, but it can look cold to some people. If other colors are cool—pink, blue, gray—white is a good trim color. A room filled with various shades of white can be gorgeous. Watch out for dirt and dust.

Cream—The choice for contrast with warm colors, such as autumn tones—browns, khaki, rust, greens, oranges. Cream is softening, less harsh than white, but also less definite. Cream is an easy-going, non-aggressive color.

Taupes and tans—Very sophisticated, these shades look great trimmed in white. They're also beautiful with black. Homes painted in shades of these colors are very livable; you won't tire of something too bold. On the other hand, they're "safe" colors that don't express much personality.

Yellow—The saying goes, "It's hard to be unhappy in a yellow room." Upbeat, sunny, and cheerful, yellow is a mood lifter, a smile-maker. Yellow is a great accent color for a blue-and-white scheme. If lemon yellow is too bright for you, check out the deeper, buttery yellows of Provence fabrics and ceramics.

Orange—Bold and risk-taking, orange is definitely "out there." It goes in and out of style, as do shades of it, such as peach. Because it's such a strong color, a little goes a long way. Orange symbolizes financial success.

Red—Red is high energy. It can be aggressive, adventurous, and in-control. Red symbolizes the blood of the battlefield, but also passion and romance. Because it's a pure color, it goes well with many others, especially as an accent tone. Some experts say every living room should have a touch of red in it. Red and yellow also increase our appetite—that's why you see them so often in fast-food restaurants.

Pink—Pink can create coolness or warmth, depending on the shade you choose. It's decidedly feminine, but pleases both men's and women's eyes. It's soft, and it reminds us of cotton candy, baby girls, roses, and lemonade—all good things. Pink is a popular way to brighten a room.

Purple—Lovers of purple swear it's the most beautiful shade there is, and if you love it, go for it (just be ready for your more timid friends to gasp when they walk in). Lavenders are restful, deep purples are rich and luxurious. Purple is the symbol of royalty. An especially dramatic combination is purple and red (you often see it at Christmas), kind of a fringed lamp shade, Casbah effect. One of the prettiest homes I've seen has eggplant-colored furniture and beautiful purple hydrangea wallpaper on a yellow background. The purple is muted and soft, not glaring, so it works.

Blue—The most popular color in the world, blue conveys relaxation and coolness. It's easy to decorate with some shade of it, and it symbolizes loyalty, patriotism, and health (notice how often it's used in medical buildings). Calming and comfortable, blue is invigorating, yet easy to live with, and it's easy to mix with other colors for a change of pace.

Green—A decorator friend of mine says forest green is the best color for carpet because it's the one color that goes with everything. And it does! (Although dark carpets show lint more than medium tones, and thus need more frequent vacuuming.) Many shades of green are soothing, like blue is. Since green is found in leaves and trees, it's a good companion color for pinks, reds, and other floral shades. It symbolizes new life, growing and living, and of course, money.

Black—I've heard that people who have the most confidence drive black cars. Who knows? Black is, of course, the strongest color you can choose, and therefore I advise using it sparingly. But I do like the distinction it brings to a room, and the zing it gives contrasting colors. Though too much can be heavy and depressing, black is nevertheless a classic and is easy to work with.

Adorning the Walls

Framed family photos—especially sepia-toned pictures of ancestors—can make a nice grouping on the wall. Other good things to frame from your family's past include such things as a tatted handkerchief, a fountain-penned letter, a string of pearls, military medals, and my favorite—antique baby clothes (use acid-free materials for the backing and matting). Not only does this preserve cherished belongings, but it displays them for all to enjoy.

I've seen great architectural statements made by a grouping of empty frames—all glossy white against a colored wall—and also by various framed mirrors arranged together.

A wall in our family room is covered with family pictures, a great way to enjoy memories and mark life's fun moments and passages.

Plan picture groupings on the floor, so you can try out different arrangements. Measure, then hang.

Do you have children or nieces or nephews? Children's art is always in style, and you can frame their efforts beautifully, not only to decorate your home, but to give the children a great sense of accomplishment.

I always enjoy seeing "things" on walls when I visit friends—a pair of crossed antique skis, a collection of baskets, folk art, quilts, African masks, Indian headdresses, weavings, awards, a rustic wooden box with something interesting inside, a wagon, a wooden swan, a giant clock. One of my pals has a gorgeous wall display above her piano of scrolls of music and musical instruments.

We have two refrigerators that we place side by side, and there's a good deal of wall space above them. We hung a black, antique bicycle there (the kind with the huge front wheel), and I like its dramatic effect against a white wall.

Tip: When hanging pictures, a good way to keep from hitting your thumb with the hammer is to hold the nail in place using an old fork.

Don't forget to make a visual splash in the kitchen. A large chalkboard mounted on the wall is a great way to utilize wall space—and to keep a running grocery list. Menu boards are also fun for posting dinners (or saving messages).

My brother-in-law and his wife have a collection of framed menus from restaurants where they've dined around the world. Framed family recipes are another inexpensive way to fill a wall. Any collection—rolling pins, butter molds, fifties diner memorabilia, cookie cutters or jars, colorful bowls—can add visual interest to your cooking domain (just remember that less clutter means less dusting).

I had a garden-themed kitchen once, and used a painted watering can for holding spatulas, whisks, and wooden spoons. I hung garden implements, birdhouses, and a wide-brimmed gardening hat on the wall. I also created a garden-themed wreath with tiny tools and pots on it. Today I have a few of those garden items in a guest bath—displayed on a gardening cart that hangs on the wall as a shelf unit. The watering can is mounted on the wall and holds towels (and a small bunny peeking out).

One of the cutest doorknobs I've ever seen was on a gift shop door—it was a gardening spade nailed to the door so that you pulled the handle to open it. Smaller versions would make clever cabinet knobs.

If you're short of cupboard space, look at baker's racks and other free-standing pie keepers and shelf units. The more unusual, the better.

How about using some creativity in the bathrooms? Another good friend has an artistic flair and hand-painted vines in hers, winding right up onto the ceiling.

My friend with the musical instruments on her wall has a gorgeous guest bath with a treasure box on the back of the toilet, draped with pearls and gems (and inside—toilet paper!)

I once hung an English horn on the wall in a bathroom and used it as a towel rack. I can't tell you how many guests found it irresistible to honk it.

Touch

Even if your tastes are stainless steel and cool surfaces, you need a cozy place to read, or just to curl up and think. Be sure you have a soft-textured wrap or blanket for cuddling in, and a comfy chair where you can get lost for a couple of hours. Schedule some down time for yourself, sip a cup of cocoa, and read a magazine. Or settle into a bubble bath with candlelight and skin-softening crystals. Designate some areas of your home for relaxation and renewal.

If you have a fireplace, and you know how to make a fire, you'll enjoy many a cozy evening. If yours is a gas fireplace, that's the easiest of all. The first step is to open the damper. Use artificial logs for zero cleanup; pressed starter logs from the supermarket are another easy option. Get a flame gun or use a very long match, and light the wrappers of the logs. Now slowly turn on the gas valve. It should flame right up. Cover with a screen.

If not using gas, starter logs are still easy; just light the wrappers and they take care of themselves. If you want to build a real old-fashioned fire, do the following: Open the damper. Gather dry, seasoned wood and twigs (or rolls of newspaper), and place them on the grate. Cover with larger logs, placing two large logs on the bottom, then another on top, at an angle. Make sure plenty of air can circulate around the wood. Now, using a flame gun or a long match, light the kindling and blow just slightly to fan the flame. Close the fireplace screen. The flames from the kindling will spread through the logs, and you'll soon have a crackling fire.

> **Tip**
> Never burn a Christmas tree in your fireplace; it can explode.

Index